MW01120628

The Theory and Interpretation of Narrative Series

James Phelan and Peter J. Rabinowitz, Editors

Psychological Politics of the American Dream

The Commodification of Subjectivity in Twentieth-Century American Literature

Lois Tyson

4-17-01

For njcate,
Who will someday,
I trust, know exactly
how truly exceptional she is).

Lois Tyson

Ohio State University Press
Columbus

Library of Congress Cataloging-in-Publication Data

Tyson, Lois, 1950–
    Psychological politics of the American dream : the commodification of
subjectivity in twentieth-century American literature / Lois Tyson.
        p. cm. — (The Theory and interpretation of narrative series)
    Includes bibliographical references and index.
    ISBN 0–8142–0626–3
        1. American literature—20th century—History and criticism—Theory, etc.
    2. Politics and literature—United States—History—20th century.
    3. Subjectivity in literature. 4. Psychology in literature. 5. Narration (Rhetoric)
    I. Title. II. Series.
    PS228.P6T97   1994
    810.9′005—dc20   93–34069
                                                      CIP

Text design by John Delaine.
Type set in Palatino and Franklin Gothic.
Printed by Braun-Brumfield, Inc., Ann Arbor, MI.

The paper in this book meets the guidelines for permanence and durability of the
Committee on Production Guidelines for Book Longevity of the Council on Library
Resources.

9   8   7   6   5   4   3   2   1

To Walter Davis

True love waits.
   —*Buddy Holly*

Contents

Acknowledgments

I would like to thank James Phelan and Peter Rabinowitz for their careful reading and very helpful suggestions in the preparation of this manuscript. Very special thanks go to Walter Davis and James Phelan for their sustained interest and good nature in guiding me through the various incarnations of this work and to Grand Valley State University for its continued financial and moral support of my endeavors. To my parents, Marie and Charles Tyson, I wish to express my gratitude for teaching me the importance of independent thinking and for having the patience to put up with me when I exercised it. Deepest appreciation is expressed for Toni Morrison, William Faulkner, Ella Fitzgerald, Ray Charles, Jean-Paul Sartre, Vincent van Gogh, and all the artists, known and unknown, whose work has made our enterprise possible and whose spirit has given our species something to shoot for.

Introduction

Subjectivity, Psychological Politics, and the American Dream

In his 1970 essay, "Ideology and Ideological State Apparatuses," Louis Althusser argues that, in order for any social system to survive, its conditions of production must be reproduced in the individual psyche. This task, he observes, is accomplished by ideology: "Ideology has the function (which defines it) of 'constituting' concrete individuals as [social] subjects" (171). To choose the simplest example, members of a capitalist society must believe, among other things, that private enterprise, individual ownership of property, and competition for wages and markets is right or natural or in their best interest; members of a communist society must believe the same about collective regulation of these economic entities. Without such ideological collusion on the part of individual members, the society as a whole could not maintain its status quo. *How* ideology fulfills its purpose—what psychological processes are involved and why they often succeed on such a large scale—has remained, however, an open question.

This question is one that we can begin to answer through literary analysis. Because literature is a repository of both a society's ideologies and its psychological conflicts, it has the capacity to reveal aspects of a culture's collective psyche, an apprehension of how ideological investments reveal the nature of individuals' psychological relationship to their world. While it is reasonable to assume that our national literature can suggest some promising hypotheses concerning the interaction of the psychological and ideological dimensions of American life, critics of American literature—despite the theoretical focus, over the last two decades, on the social origins of subjectivity—have kept these two domains separate. Instead, an archaic notion of the individual in society has remained the dominant model for American literary criticism.

1

From F. O. Matthiessen's portrait of American Renaissance writers as literary revolutionaries committed to exploring the possibilities of a self-expression inspired by the lack of a specifically American literary tradition, to Donald Pease's provocative reconsideration of the motives of American Renaissance writers in terms of their desire for community and continuity, critics of American literature have treated the individual and the socius as interactive *but discrete* entities.

Indeed, a good deal of American literary criticism places the two in a polarized opposition in which the individual is seen primarily as the victim of American society,[1] without considering the ways in which psyche and socius are dialectically related. That is, such criticism doesn't consider the ways in which the individual psyche and its cultural milieu inhabit, reflect, and define each other in a dynamically unstable, *mutually constitutive* symbiosis. In this context, psychology is always cultural psychology and politics are always psychological politics, not because, as poststructuralism would have it, the structures of consciousness are inscribed within the processes of social signification, but because both the structures of consciousness *and* the processes of social signification are inscribed within the same dialectics of desire. That is, both terms of the dichotomy are constituted by desires that neither originate in nor grant hegemony to either term, but collapse them together within a cultural amnion that makes the separation of psyche and socius an untenable theoretical construct.

While the victim model certainly has value, it is, at best, incomplete and, at worst, reductive. For the large body of American literature that focuses on the relationship between the individual and the socius, the traditional Americanist paradigm of subjectivity has produced a canon of criticism dominated by the question, Who is responsible for the protagonist's problems, the protagonist or society?—a question that precludes our seeing the dialectical connections between psyche and socius that such works reveal. This state of affairs is less surprising, however, when we consider that recent theories of subjectivity have not provided a dialectical paradigm for subjectivity and, therefore, have not offered Americanists a real alternative to the traditional model.

The poststructuralist view of subjectivity as nothing more than a collection of cultural identifications, while it has foregrounded the ways in which the notion of an autonomous subject has been used to veil society's ideological operations, has merely swung the theoretical pendulum away from the modernist emphasis on free will to a postmodern social determinism, without radically altering the terms of the dichotomy or undermining their influence. And for obvious reasons, theories of subjectivity grounded in social determinism can do little to undermine a victim model of the individual's relation to the socius. With the growing popularity of so-called ethical criticism[2]—which seeks, among other things, to reestablish the autonomous subject—we are in danger of merely continuing to swing back and forth between these two theoretical poles. The source of our problem, however, is not our inability to choose between two theoretical extremes, but the narrowness of the models of subjectivity offered by each side. My purpose here is, therefore, twofold: (1) to argue for a new model of subjectivity to replace the archaic paradigm that still informs American literary criticism and (2) to demonstrate how the model I offer opens canonized American literature to new readings of American culture. Because literary works are concerned, first and foremost, with human experience, literary interpretation requires a theory of subjectivity adequate to the task of analyzing that experience.

Once we begin to see the ways in which the individual subject is neither wholly an autonomous agent nor merely a social product, the conceptual space thereby opened makes room, not for a return to the autonomous subject the ethical critics want to construct, but for a return to and dialectical reformulation of the existential subject, arguably the most rich and useful notion of subjectivity available, but one that was popularly misunderstood when it was initially disseminated and that has been largely neglected since the advent of poststructuralism.

As Walter Davis argues in *Inwardness and Existence: Subjectivity in/ and Hegel, Heidegger, Marx, and Freud*, existentialism, properly conceived, "transcends the social-individual dichotomy" (375, n12) that informs ongoing debates between deconstruction and traditional humanism and between Marxism and psychoanalysis. For according to an existential model, social factors may largely establish our initial identity, but as we shall see in the following chapters, they do not freeze us at that stage without our daily consent. While our options are certainly limited by the society in which we live and the circumstances of our birth, we are nevertheless responsible for how we respond to those limitations. From an existential perspective, we, alone, are finally responsible for our existence. All of the "guarantees" upon which we hang our well-being—God, human nature, rationalist belief systems, the progressive nature of time—are products of our own creation; they represent our attempts to deny the reality that we are alone in a universe that has no meaning beyond what we assign to it. There is no higher plan or essence to which human life conforms; rather, existence precedes essence, which is to say that there is no "essence" at all. There is only existence and what we make of it. We are thus "condemned" to freedom: it is up to us what we make of our lives, of our communities, of our planet.

According to Davis, if we fully submit existential subjectivity to the dialectical process implicit in the existential view of human experience, we emerge with a model of the individual as a historically situated (Marxist) subject of (psychoanalytic) desire, condemned to his or her own (existential) freedom to be either in collusion with social forces—consciously or unconsciously—or to resist. And this subjectivity is informed by what I would call a destablized Hegelianism: the dialectical relationship between the individual and the socius—like that among the Marxist, psychoanalytic, and existential realities that constitute subjectivity—does not issue in some reified *Geist*, but remains in a state of contingency and flux, anchored in the real world, utterly existentialized. A dialectical model of existential subjectivity thus merges the heretofore opposed categories in which other definitions of subjectivity have been grounded.[3]

If we apply this model of subjectivity to American literature, the question for literary critics ceases to be, Is the individual a free agent or a social product? and becomes instead, How are the individual and the socius cut from the fabric of the same desire? In other words, what are the dialectics of desire that constitute our psychological politics? What psychological payoffs, conscious or unconscious, do we seek through our acceptance of any given ideology, whether articulated or not? This theoretical perspective might be termed an existential dialectics—though Davis doesn't refer to it as such—and the following chapters will attempt to illustrate its efficacy as a framework for interpreting American literature.

Through close readings of representative works of twentieth-century American literature generally considered to portray the individual in opposition to society—Edith Wharton's *House of Mirth* (1905), F. Scott Fitzgerald's *Great Gatsby* (1925), Arthur Miller's *Death of a Salesman* (1949), Thomas Pynchon's *Crying of Lot 49* (1966), and Joseph Heller's *Something Happened* (1974)—I examine the ways in which these texts reveal instead how psyche and socius intersect in terms of the most pervasive ideological site upon which the American psyche has projected itself: the American dream. Although, in ideal terms, the American dream is a social vision in which, as James Truslow Adams put it in 1931, "each man and each woman shall be able to attain . . . the fullest stature of which they are innately capable" (374), most writers who use the phrase recognize that one's "stature" in America is usually judged as a function of one's socioeconomic status. The American dream is thus a dream of the commodity, and the implied premise is that one's spiritual worth and well-being are directly proportional to the value of the commodities one owns. As Marius Bewley observes, "Essentially, this phrase [*American dream*] represents the romantic enlargement of the possibilities of life on a level at which the material and the spiritual have become inextricably confused" (11). And as is especially clear in the case of *Death of a Salesman*'s Willy Loman, the relationship between the material and spiritual domains is seen as causal: socioeconomic status, or upward mobility, is valorized as the *source* of spiritual worth and well-being. The underlying assumption is, as Edwin Fussell notes, "that all the magic of the world can be had for money" (44), and as we see in *The Great Gatsby*, it is the impossible "meeting" of these two terms—*money* and *magic*—that defines the American dream. Furthermore, because the dream is, as Milton R. Stern puts it, "a dream of self rather than community" (166), it is especially suited to reproduce in the individual the ideology necessary for the survival of a free-enterprise, capitalist system like ours.

As these statements by Bewley, Fussell, and Stern illustrate, there is a general awareness that the American dream is an ideological structure in which material and spiritual domains are yoked in a way that promotes an unrealistic reliance on the former to the detriment of the latter. Nevertheless, many Americans believe that the American dream is not inherently corrupt but has become so over time. For example, in a dictionary of "picturesque expressions" published in 1985, *American dream* is defined as consisting originally of "the vision of attaining maximum security and fulfillment of opportunity as an individual without concern for social distinctions." This definition is then contrasted with what the dream has *become*: "Today the term is often heard cynically with an implication of distrust or as a way of characterizing an affluent way of life that often tends toward money madness" (Urdang, Hunsinger, and LaRoche 340). Similarly, Rose Adrienne Gallo, in her discussion of *The Great Gatsby*, describes an original American dream "based on ambition, industry, and well-defined rules of conduct" that "produced men of strength and character whose success contributed to the prosperity and greatness of the nation," and she contrasts it with a "vitiated American dream" that "spawned a new generation of strong men, represented by the undisciplined brute force of the Tom Buchanans, and, worse, by the unscrupulous machinations of the Meyer Wolfsheims" (54). In fact, in the criticism of such works as *The Great Gatsby* and *Death of a Salesman*, references to "the withering of the American dream" (Bewley 11) or "the deterioration of the 'American Dream'" (D. Parker 31) are too numerous to mention. Clearly, a dream can't "wither" or "deteriorate" if it wasn't, at one time, well and whole.

Ideology, however, isn't present only when we perceive it. In fact, the less we are aware of it the freer it is to operate. This is why members of both major political parties in this country can get elected to office by promising us a return to something that never existed: the American dream in its pristine form. Americans who believe that the American dream has *become* corrupt perhaps assume that the dream's corruption is as recent as their awareness of it. The irony revealed by the literature of the American dream is that, inherent in the ideological structure of the dream's equation of material and spiritual fulfillment, are the "seductive and corrupting motivations" (Fussell 46) that we have finally come to associate with it. In other words, the American dream is, inherently, a commodified dream, and it promotes commodification as a psychological stance. Indeed, as the following chapters will illustrate, the terms *American dream* and *commodity* are virtually interchangeable, for the American dream is the ideological apparatus of the commodity.

A commodity, by Karl Marx's definition, has value not in terms of what it can do (use value) but in terms of the money or other commodities for which it can be traded (exchange value) or, as the French sociologist Jean Baudrillard notes, in terms of the prestige and social status its ownership confers (sign-exchange value). An object becomes a commodity only when it has exchange value or sign-exchange value, and neither form of value is inherent in any object. Both are forms of social value: they are values *assigned* to objects by human beings in a given social context. Commodification, then, is the act or condition of relating to persons or things in terms of their exchange value or sign-exchange value to the exclusion of other considerations. The term *commodification*—unlike such related terms as *objectification* or *social status*—thus carries with it the spiritual devaluation of self and other inherent in the

American dream's marketplace psychology. While there are a number of ideological vehicles that carry among their baggage the cult of the commodity—commercial advertisements, religious beliefs, political partisanship—the American dream is the overarching myth to which such ideological vehicles refer. The American dream is itself a consumer product, which Americans "buy into" as the primary myth by means of which they mold their interpersonal relations to resemble relations of capitalist production, which are relations among commodities. Furthermore, because the dream is a dream of status, sign-exchange value becomes preeminent: exchange value and sign-exchange value are collapsed—exchange value becomes a form of sign-exchange value—and use value is disenfranchised, obliterated.

Anything can be commodified. Art can be commodified when a work is purchased solely for the price it will bring a few years hence or for the prestige of owning it. A woman's youth and beauty can be commodified, just like the jewels she is wearing. And human relationships can be commodified as well, as we can see in the following dialogue from Woody Allen's *Play It Again, Sam*, in which Dick and Linda Christie are talking with Allan Felix about the recent breakup of Allan's marriage.

> **Linda**: Oh, he really loved her. I feel like crying.
> **Dick**: Why do you feel like crying? A man makes an investment; it doesn't pay off. . . . Allan, you've invested your emotions in a losing stock. It was wiped out. It dropped off the board. Now, what do you do, Allan? You reinvest—maybe in a more stable stock—something with long-term growth possibilities.
> **Allan**: Who you gonna fix me up with, General Motors?

One obvious way in which Dick's discourse is commodified in this excerpt is that it reveals what is, in his opinion, really at stake: profit and loss—in this case, profit and loss in terms of time, emotional energy, and social status. However, another, more powerful effect of such language, and the real payoff for the speaker, is that it distances him from the objects of his discourse. Dick's real project in convincing Allan to "reinvest" is to distance himself emotionally from Allan's feelings, and to get Allan to do the same. Dick wants to increase the exchange and sign-exchange value of his friend without "investing" any of his own emotional energy. The psychology informing Dick's behavior might be termed commodity psychology, and it is not merely a theme in the literary works I will discuss but a structural principle that organizes the progression of narrative and dramatic events.

For most of us, Dick's attitude is familiar because commodity psychology has become a common way of being in the world and relating to others. It's the psychology one adopts whenever one relates to persons or things as commodities, that is, in terms of their relative worth on a market, such as the "job market" or the "marriage market." People commodify themselves and others when, for example—like Jack Green in Joseph Heller's *Something Happened*—they try to be seen at parties talking with someone whose social status is higher than theirs in order to increase their own sign-exchange value. Part of the payoff of this kind of commodity psychology is the same kind of avoidance of feeling Dick Cristie achieves: one doesn't have to deal with the needs and feelings of others or with needs and feelings of one's own that one would rather not face. While the concept of commodity psychology is certainly simple enough, its manifestations are, as we shall see, subtle, complex, and diverse.

Obviously, the American socius—in terms of its socioeconomic status quo—has long benefited from an American dream in which socioeconomic advancement is linked with spiritual worth and well-being: one can hardly imagine a vision better equipped to promote the consumption of commodities on which our culture depends or, in Althusserian terms, better suited to reproduce the ideology necessary for the survival of a capitalist system like ours. But what is the benefit to the individual, who, as Wharton, Fitzgerald, Miller, Pynchon, and Heller suggest, is spiritually withered by his or her own emotional investment in socioeconomic status? The victim model suggests that individuals subscribe to the American dream because they are manipulated or ideologically programmed to do so. This explanation, however, like the Althusserian formulation, sidesteps the question of how such manipulation occurs. As Wolfgang Haug observes, manipulation can be effective only if it has "latched on to the 'objective interests' of those being manipulated" (6). What, then, are the "objective interests" served by the American dream?

As we shall see, the American dream, through its inherent relation to commodity psychology, responds to the desire to escape existential inwardness, that anxious awareness of oneself as a creature "whose very being is at issue" (Heidegger 67) in an uncertain world. Financial worries, the inevitability of aging and death, the possibility of accident or ill-

ness, and the fear of emotional pain all number among the kinds of un-
foreseeable events—historical contingencies—that increase and compli-
cate the anxieties inherent in being human, in having a consciousness
that is aware of itself in a context of unanswerable questions: Why was I
born? What is the purpose of life? What should I believe and how
should I behave? What will happen to me after I die? When we take full
responsibility for our actions and sustain existential inwardness as the
guiding principle of our behavior, we have undertaken the existential
project to live an authentic existence. In contrast, to escape existential inwardness is to escape the awareness of historical contingency and the
responsibility to respond to it conscientiously. This escape is accomplished through what Jean-Paul Sartre calls bad faith (*mauvaise foi*), the
various lies we tell ourselves in order to shift the responsibility for our
own actions onto persons or forces outside ourselves.

While I'm not arguing that the flight from existential inwardness is an
essential, or timeless, quality of human nature—an existential framework does not permit essentialism and, therefore, doesn't recognize human "nature"—neither am I suggesting that the desire to escape
existential inwardness is socially produced, at least not in the way a doc-
trinaire Marxist would use the phrase. Instead, I'm trying to demonstrate the need for a whole new way of understanding what it means for
phenomena to be socially produced that does not posit an *abstract* social
formation *independent* of individual desire. Therefore, the flight from existential inwardness—and indeed, all the theoretical concepts employed
here—are treated phenomenologically: my attempt is to *describe* the
ways in which psychological and ideological phenomena merge, rather
than to posit an essentialist or constructionist final cause. Indeed, my
paradigm of subjectivity is based on the collapse of this dichotomy.
Thus, for example, the psychoanalytic concepts used in this study do not
assume the essentialist status some psychoanalytic theorists accord
them; neither do the Marxist concepts I employ assume the constructionist status some Marxist theorists accord them. I operate, instead,
from the assumption that there is no such thing as purely psychological
or purely ideological phenomena: all psychological phenomena are
ideological as well, just as all ideological phenomena are also psychological, because both domains issue from the merger of individual and
institutionalized desire. This does not mean that there is no such thing as
an individual victim of institutionalized oppression. It means, instead,
that sustained, "successful" institutionalized oppression bespeaks a cul-

tural psychology that (consciously or unconsciously) supports it, even among those who are (knowingly or unknowingly) victimized. The sources and characteristics of such a cultural psychology are often difficult to see precisely because psychological politics do not rest upon and cannot be explained by structural principles that compartmentalize human experience in an effort to explain it. Attempts to place the final cause of human behavior in either the essentialist or the constructionist domain have failed to articulate an adequate model of subjectivity because they rely, by definition, on such compartmentalization.

In the chapters that follow, we will see how individual and institutionalized desire, in twentieth-century America, merge in the commodity. The desire to escape existential inwardness is inextricably linked to the commodity through displacement and mystification: one displaces all one's anxieties onto the commodity in the belief that the commodity will somehow magically make one "happy," that is, provide the illusion that one has transcended historical contingency. In other words, each purchase is an emblem not merely of one's sign-exchange value but of one's self-reification as substance, as that which is, paradoxically, both nonexistent and immortal. At most, of course, one's purchases (of commodities, of social status, of human relationships) merely provide a fleeting illusion of transcendence that therefore requires continual reinforcement (one must always buy a bigger house or acquire membership in a more exclusive social set) and bad faith (one must find specious reasons for one's purchases and social climbing) to avoid facing the real motivation behind the obsessive desire to accumulate wealth and status. This is the transcendental project—the desire to escape existential inwardness—informing the psychological events that structure the five works I examine. My intention is not to investigate the sociohistorical circumstances of the texts' production—a worthwhile project, but one beyond the scope and purpose of this one—but to examine the psychosocial operations implicit in their representations of human behavior.

While the victim model lets subjectivity off the hook of existential responsibility, a dialectical model permits me to put it back on. Thus, Edith Wharton's *House of Mirth* is read in terms of what it reveals about the psychological payoffs for both genders for their investment in a principal avatar of the American dream: woman as aesthetic commodity fetish. I argue that the protagonist attempts to escape existential inwardness through self-reification as an aesthetic object and that her problematical death at the novel's close is, for both her and her male counterpart, the consummation of their delusional transcendental project. F. Scott Fitzgerald's *Great Gatsby* is analyzed in terms of the commodification of identity promoted by the American dream. Here the flight from existential inwardness is manifest both in the protagonist's attempt to cancel his identity by escaping into a fictionalized past and in the "subject-object" model of interpersonal relations that is the novel's dominant value and the "object-object" model that is its emergent value.[4]

Arthur Miller's *Death of a Salesman* is used to show how the American dream provides the "ore" from which individuals can fashion an ideological armor to disguise and deny their true psychological state. In this case, the flight from existential inwardness is revealed in what I argue are the five regressive episodes that structure the play, as well as in the Loman family's sexuality, which is an important, though critically neglected, aspect of this work. In Thomas Pynchon's *Crying of Lot 49*, we find an American dream that blatantly invites psychological investment in an ideological surface the purpose of which is to cancel all interiority. This novel is examined in terms of the question, Can existential subjectivity still constitute itself once the individual and the socius are symbiotically dissolved in the self-emptying commodity signs that constitute the contemporary American dream? Here the flight from existential inwardness is a cultural fait accompli, and the possibilities of its reconstruction in contemporary America are put on trial.

Finally, Joseph Heller's *Something Happened* is analyzed to suggest the ways in which contemporary American subjectivity uses the American dream, in this case, the ideology of the corporate commodity, to move beyond the existential problematic. In this novel, the flight from existential inwardness is not merely attempted but accomplished: the protagonist deliberately and consciously—without bad faith as a psychological crutch—commodifies his own consciousness on the corporate model, reducing his psychological experience to the kinds of abstract relations that obtain among commodities in late capitalist culture.[5] Taken together, these works outline a psychology of the commodity that is a psychology of repression, regression, and death. Viewed chronologically, the texts point to a growing collusion of psyche and socius: the desire to escape existential inwardness becomes an increasingly "viable" project with the increasing commodification of our national culture.

In addition to the thematic focus outlined above, the American dream's ideological power is examined in terms of its ability to seduce authors and critics. For example, I argue that *The Great Gatsby*'s critique of commodity psychology is inadvertently undercut by the seductive appeal with which Fitzgerald portrays the commodity. This appeal, I suggest, helps to seduce the many critics who rally to Gatsby's cause because of a desire to protect their ideological investment in an American dream of their own. Similarly, I maintain that Miller unconsciously tries to sabotage the rich psychological subtexts that make his work the masterpiece it is by manipulating the play's formal elements to foreground an overly sympathetic reading of his protagonist. The play's critics, I argue, have responded to Miller's desire, and to their own identification with the protagonist's project, by finding Willy Loman both the victim and the tragic hero that Miller wants him to be.

The collapse of the psychological and ideological dimensions of these five works implies a psychological politics grounded in a thoroughly existentialized dialectic of psyche and socius, for as I suggested earlier, it shows that the structures of consciousness and the processes of social signification are inscribed within the same dialectics of desire and that this inscription does not fit the victim model of the relationship between the individual and the socius that, explicitly or implicitly, still informs American literary criticism. If Americans are manipulated by the ideology of the American dream, it is because that ideology is so easily manipulated to serve our own psychological ends. And surely it is here—in the nature of the psychological payoffs offered by the adherence to a belief system—that the seductive power of ideology in general, and of the American dream in particular, really lies. If we want to continue to examine the ways in which American literature places the individual in opposition to society, we must interrogate this dichotomization of psyche and socius by analyzing the ways in which our literature reveals the dialectical complexities of their inexorable existential symbiosis.

In keeping with the dialectical notion of subjectivity that informs this investigation, I analyze the literary texts I have chosen using Marxist, psychoanalytic, existentialist, feminist, and poststructuralist critical tools in dialectical conjunction. Unlike interpretation that occurs within a Kantian set of assumptions, wherein the final goal is to sift the literary text through a series of totalizing categories, a dialectical approach privileges a totalizing *process* in which categories remain fluid and, themselves, in process. Thus, theoretical categories can be used together, as different-color threads are woven to make a fabric that cannot be named for any single color used in its composition. Indeed, as the following chapters illustrate, a dialectical paradigm of subjectivity encourages dialectical interplay among critical theories. For example, a dialectical approach, as we shall see, illustrates how critical tools from a number of different nonformalist schools can be used together to produce what New Critics would consider unified, close readings. In fact, this method makes it possible to account for many textual elements that are inadequately addressed or overlooked entirely in other readings of these same works.

Of course, not every theory is used equally to solve every interpretive problem. In fact, the dialectical approach will be best understood if we think of it not in terms of full-blown theoretical frameworks, such as Marxism, psychoanalysis, existentialism, feminism, and deconstruction, but in terms of individual theoretical concepts—such as commodification, regression, existential inwardness, the fetishization of women, and our epistemological reliance on binary oppositions—that may have originated within one theoretical framework but that can be put in service of another or combined with concepts from several other frameworks to perform the interpretive task at hand, however large or small that task may be. What concepts are used and in what combination will depend on both the individual reader's purpose and personal preference. There is no set formula: what may work best in one given interpretive context, or for one particular reader, may not work best in another context or for another reader. The process is very much akin to *bricolage*, a concept Derrida adapted from Claude Lévi-Strauss: the use of the best tools available to perform the task at hand, regardless of the original purpose for which any given tool was constructed.

In the following chapters, existentialism provides the grounding concepts in service of which all other theoretical concepts perform because the overarching theme of this study is the flight from existential inwardness, which, I argue, forms the foundation of the American dream's psychological politics, in other words, the fundamental psychological attraction of the American dream's ideological program. Thus, concepts such as commodification, regression, and the fetishization of women are all examined in terms of how they facilitate the flight from existential inwardness. And each concept was chosen—often by trial and error—to perform a particular interpretive task because the textual meaning it produced deepened my understanding of some relevant psychosocial phenomenon explicit or implicit in a given literary representation of human behavior.

Of course, from the standpoint of my paradigm of subjectivity, one could argue that deconstruction provides the grounding concepts for this study, in that my reading of mainstream American literature, and of the critical canon that has interpreted it, is based upon the deconstruction of the traditional binary opposition between social determinism and free will. There are a number of theoretical vantage points within a dialectical reading from which to view the act of interpretation because a dialectical approach is kaleidoscopic rather than linear: it is very fluid, interactive, open-ended, nonformulaic. Thus, although such an approach has the capacity to be rather anxiety producing, it also has the capacity to be very fertile, rearranging old assumptions within startling new configurations.

A dialectical approach, moreover, encourages an interplay between critical theories and literary texts that can help us see the limitations of literary and philosophical concepts too often employed uncritically. For example, in my chapter on *The Great Gatsby* I attempt to problematize the notion of the reliable narrator by suggesting that this concept is grounded in an untenable concept of the reliable author. And my reading of *Something Happened* points out the limitations of a Sartrean notion of subjectivity for contemporary experience: the existential framework implicit in the common assumption of Slocum's bad faith is, in fact, unable to contain the protagonist's experience. (Thus, a dialectical approach can call into question even those concepts associated with the theoretical framework one is employing.) In addition, I use this novel's understanding of human behavior to extend Jean Baudrillard's theory of sign-exchange value, a theory central to the concept of commodification that informs all five chapters. Such an interplay of theoretical and literary texts demonstrates how these works can "read" one another, thereby problematizing the privileged use of any one theoretical framework to understand literature and obviating the debate among academicians concerning the primacy of either critical theory or literature for understanding the human condition.

This collapse of some of the distinctions between literary and theoretical texts is a corollary of my working definition of literature, which is related both to poststructuralism and to reader-response theory. For me, a literary text is a site of cultural/psychological events—both in its original composition and in the act of reading. As Stanley Fish notes, the boundaries of the physical pages mislead us into thinking that the text itself is bounded (82) when, in fact, it's a piece of living history, an anthropological artifact, that reads not only the individuals who produce and interpret it—authors and critics—but also the cultures in which it is produced and interpreted. Thus, any given text contains the possibility of any number of different readings—some compatible, some not—at any given moment as well as over time. My interest lies not in which reading/readings is/are "correct," even if such a conclusion could be drawn, but in how different readings use the text to teach us something about human experience and how one reading can be used to arrest or limit the insights of another.

Of course, any attempt to outline a critical methodology requires that attention be given to the problem of author and authorial intention. Certainly, the intentionalist notion of the author as an artist who manipulates the text exclusively in a deliberate, conscious, and rational manner—the author with whom the reliable narrator is in accord—is a very limited and limiting, if not untenable, concept. While any given intentionalist reading may be as useful as any other given reading, the intentionalist desire is one that seeks a kind of textual closure that often works against interpretive possibility. A more useful and, I think, accurate formulation is the notion of the author as a conflicted, ideologically saturated artist driven by motives, both conscious and unconscious, too numerous and complicated to be a factor in her or his conscious creation of the text. Even when authors comment on their own work, as they so often do, their statements of intention provide us merely with one additional interpretation of their work, an interpretation that should be submitted to the same criteria by which we evaluate any other critical reading. For while an author's intentions certainly play an important role—for example, in the stylistic and thematic choices that structure the work—the narrative is often constituted in a much more powerful way by what the author might not want to tell us or might not know. Thus the reliable narrator, when this function can be established, has but a limited story to tell.

The literature of the American dream, however, tells a story without limits, a story of excess and of excesses, in which "limit and deprivation are [the] blackest devils" (Bewley 12). Of course, the five literary works examined in the following chapters represent rather than exhaust the works of twentieth-century American literature that illuminate the psychological politics of the American dream. The texts I've chosen are offered as test cases, so to speak: mainstream literary works, spanning the century, that, like most mainstream literature, have engendered a canon of criticism almost as useful as the literary texts themselves in providing material for analysis. Most important, however, these five works illustrate the diversity and complexity of the psychosocial realities American literature can reveal, given a model of subjectivity adequate to the task.

1

Woman as Fetish

Self-Reification and the Aesthetic Commodity in Edith Wharton's *House of Mirth*

Edith Wharton explored the relationship between the individual and the socius through issues of class and gender as they were manifested during one of America's most explosive periods of industrial expansion and exploitation. As Blake Nevius observes, "Edith Wharton was one of the first American novelists to develop the possibilities of a theme which since the turn of the century has permeated our fiction: the waste of human and spiritual resources which in America went hand in hand with the exploitation of the land and forests" (55). The "exploitation of the land and forests" to which Nevius refers hit a high point during the post–Civil War industrial boom that made the fortunes of men like *The Great Gatsby's* Dan Cody and *The House of Mirth's* Gus Trenor, George Dorset, and Simon Rosedale. It was a time when get-rich-quick schemes proliferated, and the possibilities for fulfilling the American dream seemed to expand as rapidly as the nation's borders. Of course, the "waste of human and spiritual resources" that accompanied this expansion included the waste of America's womanhood, and in Wharton's novels this theme is central. In both *The Custom of the Country* (1913) and *The Age of Innocence* (1920), for example, women are represented as marriage commodities who sell themselves to the highest bidder in their attempt to move up the American dream's socioeconomic ladder. However, few works—in Wharton's corpus or elsewhere—treat the issue of woman as commodity as thoroughly as her first major novel, *The House of Mirth* (1905), a chilling portrait of wealthy New York society at the turn of the century.

While readers disagree in their interpretations of some aspects of protagonist Lily Bart,[1] most see her as a heroic figure who is morally superior to the socius whose victim she becomes. As Margaret B. McDowell puts it, "New York society was nefarious . . . precisely because it debased an individual like Lily Bart" (43), an individual whose "moral appeal," Susan Goodman argues, "stems from her persistent refusal to define herself as a commodity" (50). A beautiful, intelligent young woman who hasn't the money to support herself in the stratum of high society to which she was born and bred, Lily must rely upon her beauty and social graces in order to keep her position in the Trenor-Dorset milieu. Although she is twenty-nine years old when the novel opens—and should therefore lose no more time in acquiring the rich husband she needs in order to put a permanent end to her financial problems—Lily cannot bring herself to marry the dull, self-involved species of male, such as Percy Gryce, who has the money, if not the spirit, to keep her in the high style she requires. We learn, in fact, that the protagonist has spent the eleven years since her debut avoiding marriage to a number of rich men for whom she had successfully "set her cap." A series of social difficulties, in which Lily figures as the victim of unscrupulous society figures Gus Trenor and Bertha Dorset, sends her into a severe social and financial decline. Unwilling, because of the higher vision of life awakened in her by Lawrence Selden, to reestablish her position through the morally questionable means at her disposal (the quiet purchase of Bertha Dorset's good will through the use of some indiscreet letters written by that lady, followed by marriage to Simon Rosedale), Lily sinks further and further into poverty and despair and finally dies from an overdose of a sleeping drug.

This interpretation of the novel forms the core of a critical consensus that leaves several important questions—related both to our understanding of the protagonist and to the novel's narrative progression—inadequately answered. Given that the wealthy life-style she requires is available in more than one stratum of society, what is behind Lily's idée fixe that she must have a place in the relatively small world of the Trenors and Dorsets? Why doesn't she finally marry to achieve the financial and social stability she seeks? What is the source of Lawrence Selden's power over her? What is the source, in the final chapters of the novel, of the apparent hypermorality for which the protagonist sacrifices every possibility of survival? What is the significance of her death?

Most critics answer these questions in terms of what they believe is the moral opposition of the two worlds between which Lily vacillates: the superficial, commodified world of the Trenor-Dorset milieu and the rarefied, spiritual world she associates with Lawrence Selden. Despite some critical antipathy to Selden, who, as Cynthia Griffin Wolff puts it, is "a mouthpiece for the worst of society's prejudices" (111), what is seen as the protagonist's growing moral fiber is linked with her growing interest in him. Lily's "spiritual needs," Roslyn Dixon argues, are what "draw her to Selden" (218). While Selden may not be worthy of Lily's admiration, her feelings for him are credited with the ethical concerns for which she sacrifices not only her last chance to return to fashionable society but the last of her financial resources as well. As Elaine Showalter notes, "Lawrence Selden . . . demands . . . [a] moral perfection that [Lily] can finally only satisfy by dying" (35).[2]

However, if we replace the victim model of the relationship between the individual and the socius, which has informed most readings of this novel, with a dialectical model of subjectivity, which foregrounds the ways in which individual desire and social formations coincide, we can see that the critical focus on Lily Bart's moral dimension misses the novel's analysis of a subtler phenomenon that collapses the opposition between the Trenor-Dorset weltanschauung and the alternative Lily sees in Lawrence Selden: the psychology of woman as commodity fetish, a principal avatar of the American dream. This chapter will attempt to show that *The House of Mirth* dramatizes the psychological contradictions and dead ends to which a woman's transcendental project—her labor to escape existential inwardness through self-reification—is liable in our culture. Lily doesn't "resis[t] reification" (92), as Dale Bauer maintains; as we shall see, she actively seeks it. Her project is to become an objet d'art, not as a transgressive act of self-authorship, as Bauer forcefully argues (97), but in order to escape existential inwardness.[3] I will argue that Lawrence Selden finally exerts the more powerful influence on Lily, not because he offers her an alternative to this goal, but because he offers her, through a parallel project of his own, the more effective means of achieving it.

Most readers easily recognize that the world of the Trenors and the Dorsets, among whom Lily has cast her lot, is a marketplace where women number among the commodities for sale.[4] Lily was raised to succeed in this world by being its best commodity. Her mother

> studied [Lily's beauty] with a kind of passion, as though it were some
> weapon she had slowly fashioned for her vengeance [for having lost her
> money and, therefore, her social standing]. It was the last asset in their
> fortunes, the nucleus around which their life was to be rebuilt. She
> watched it jealously, as though it were her own property and Lily its

mere custodian; and she tried to instil into the latter a sense of the responsibility that such a charge involved. She followed in imagination the career of other beauties, pointing out to her daughter what might be achieved through such a gift, and dwelling on the awful warning of those who, in spite of it, had failed to get what they wanted. (35–36; bk. 1, ch. 3)

The individuals with whom Lily socializes prove Mrs. Bart to have been right in her assessment of high society.[5] Percy Gryce would like to marry Lily for the same reason he likes being the owner of the Gryce Americana: she is an eminently collectible item that will gain him the attention and envy of his peers (51; bk. 1, ch. 4). Simon Rosedale—an extremely wealthy aspirant to the world of the Trenors and the Dorsets, who, it seems inevitable, will ultimately be accepted into that group—is attracted to Lily because of "his collector's passion for the rare and unattainable" (119; bk. 1, ch. 10); he wants the sign-exchange value he would get from the possession of a wife who could "make all the other women feel small" (185; bk. 1, ch. 15). Mrs. Wellington Bry, among the more recent pretenders to the Trenor-Dorset clique, desires Lily's company during her tour of Mediterranean watering places because she believes that Lily can secure her the introduction she seeks into the European aristocratic set (209; bk. 2, ch. 2).

Although more intelligent and sensitive than most members of her group, Lily commodifies people just as they do. She wonders, for example, why Selden "had always been kind to his dull cousin [Gerty Farish] . . . why he wasted so much time in such an unremunerative manner" (94; bk. 1, ch. 8). Similarly, Lily doesn't accord her poor and unattractive cousin Grace Stepney the "scant civilities . . . [she] accorded to Mr. Rosedale" because she did not "foresee that such a friend [as Grace] was worth cultivating" (128; bk. 1, ch. 11). Most important for our purposes, Lily commodifies herself.

As a commodity, Lily has fashioned herself to resemble one of the rarest and most expensive items on the market: the objet d'art. Her appearance as a tableau vivant of Reynolds's "Mrs. Lloyd" at the Wellington Bry entertainment epitomizes her concept of herself as an art object. As Lily is well aware,

The unanimous "Oh!" of the spectators was a tribute, not to the brushwork of Reynolds's "Mrs. Lloyd" but to the flesh and blood loveliness of Lily Bart. . . . It was as though she had stepped, not out of, but into, Reynolds's canvas, banishing the phantom of his dead beauty by the

beams of her living grace. . . . she had purposely chosen a picture without distracting accessories of dress or surroundings. Her pale draperies,
and the background of foliage against which she stood, served only to
relieve the long dryad-like curves that swept upward from her poised
foot to her lifted arm. (141–42; bk. 1, ch. 12)

Lily is as much a tableau vivant in the daily routine of her social life
as she is in her representation of Reynolds's portrait. Always wanting
to produce an effect of idealized beauty, Lily is very deliberate in her
exploitation, not just of costume, but of facial expression and setting as
well. As she leans against the ballustrade of the terrace at Bellomont, for
example, she notes that Percy Gryce has spotted her from the midst of
his reluctant tête à tête with Mrs. Fisher. "He cast agonized glances in
the direction of Miss Bart, whose only response was to sink into an attitude of more graceful abstraction. She had learned the value of contrast
in throwing her charms into relief, and was fully aware of the extent to
which Mrs. Fisher's volubility was enhancing her own repose" (49; bk.
1, ch. 4).

Similarly, the life-style she desires for herself would be a "frame" for
the display of her beauty: like Annie's desire for "perfect moments" in
Sartre's *Nausea*, "the life [Lily] longed to lead [was one] in which every
detail should have the finish of a jewel, and the whole form a harmonious setting to her own jewel-like rareness" (94; bk. 1, ch. 8). Thus, she
dreams of living in "an apartment which should surpass the complicated luxury of her friends' surroundings by the whole extent of that artistic sensibility which made her feel herself their superior; in which
every tint and line should combine to enhance her beauty and give distinction to her leisure!" (115; bk. 1, ch. 9). Even nature is reduced to the
function of frame and put in the service of Lily's desire to fashion herself as an aesthetic commodity: during a solitary walk in the woods
near Bellomont, she finds a "charming" spot, "and Lily was not insen-
sible to the charm, or to the fact that her presence enhanced it; but she
was not accustomed to taste the joys of solitude except in company, and
the combination of a handsome girl and a romantic scene struck her as
too good to be wasted" (63; bk. 1, ch. 5).

It is this aspect of commodification—Lily's conception and treatment
of herself as an aesthetic commodity—that is most important for our
understanding of her psychology. And it is her psychology that must be
explored if we are to find sufficient motivation for behaviors that ulti-

mately result in the protagonist's social and financial downfall, beginning with her decision to try to retain, at all costs, her membership in the Trenor-Dorset milieu.

Wharton gives us a number of reasons for Lily Bart's idée fixe that the only world in which she can be happy is the narrow social stratum led by the Trenors and the Dorsets. As a young girl, she was socialized into the world of ease and plenty by her mother, who brought her up to be "ornamental" (313; bk. 2, ch. 11), to be beautiful and well versed in the social graces and little else. Therefore, Lily's skills suit her for two occupations only: making herself useful to wealthy society hostesses and attracting a wealthy husband. In addition, many critics believe, as Lily herself does, that her desire to remain a member of this world is related to an appreciation for beauty that manifests itself as a deep-seated need to be around lovely things:[6] "An atmosphere of luxury . . . was the background she required, the only climate she could breathe in" (27; bk. 1, ch. 3). "She knew that she hated dinginess as much as her mother had hated it" (40; bk. 1, ch. 3), while "she felt an affinity to all the subtler manifestations of wealth" that she enjoyed at Bellomont in "the studied luxury" of, for example, "her breakfast tray, with its harmonious porcelain and silver, a handful of violets in a slender glass, and the morning paper folded beneath her letters" (41; bk. 1, ch. 4).

There are, however, wealthy hostesses and eligible bachelors in strata of society other than that of the Trenors and the Dorsets. Indeed, the Sam Gormers have as much money as many of the members of the Trenor-Dorset set, and they are willing to afford Lily the same material upkeep and the same beautiful surroundings she requires. Moreover, at the Gormers, there is "a greater good-nature, less rivalry, and a fresher capacity for enjoyment" (244; bk. 2, ch. 5). In fact, the Gormers don't impose upon Lily the chafing little tasks—the obligation to entertain boring guests and bored husbands, to perform secretarial tasks when asked, and to play bridge for stakes she cannot afford—the Trenor-Dorset clan requires of her in exchange for their patronage. Yet, for Lily, only the world of the Trenors and Dorsets will do. When her fortunes decline and she finds herself socializing with the Gormers, she desperately seeks to return to her former group. Certainly, it isn't a case of nostalgia for old friends and good times that makes the protagonist long for her old clique: Lily has been deeply hurt by Bertha Dorset and Judy Trenor, the only two women in that group with whom she had spent much time. And it's not likely that the consideration of social standing alone is the reason behind Lily's dissatisfaction with her new, somewhat less prominent milieu. For even the stigma of *nouveaux arrivés* won't cling to the Gormers for long in a society in which, as Lily herself observes, "social credit" is "based on an impregnable bank-account" (274; bk. 2, ch. 8).

There is, however, one thing the Trenor-Dorset clique can provide that the Gormers don't, and it's something that a "superfine human merchandise" (268; bk. 2, ch. 7) like Lily can't resist: a more discriminating appreciation for her exchange value. At the Sam Gormers, "Lily had the odd sense of being caught up into the crowd as carelessly as a passenger is gathered in by an express train" (244; bk. 2, ch. 5):

> Miss Bart's arrival had been welcomed with an uncritical friendliness that first irritated her pride and then brought her to a sharp sense of her own situation. . . . These people knew her story—of that her first long talk with Carry Fisher had left no doubt: she was publicly branded as the heroine of a "queer" episode—but instead of shrinking from her as her own friends had done, they received her without question into the easy promiscuity of their lives. They swallowed her past as easily as they did Miss Anstell's [an actress of unknown origin], and with no apparent sense of any difference in the size of the mouthful. (245; bk. 2, ch. 5)

In contrast, the Trenor-Dorset clan is very discriminating in their appraisal of associates—they're used to the best human commodities available, and they make fine distinctions among them. Although people like the Wellington Brys and Simon Rosedale—owing to the strategic use of their great wealth—manage to increase their social exchange value to the point where the Trenor-Dorset set accepts them, Lily knows that they can never receive "that precise note of approval" that a woman of her abilities is capable of calling forth (143; bk. 1, ch. 12). As an aesthetic commodity long devoted to the attainment and maintenance of her position at the market's "top of the line," the protagonist must display herself before a company who knows exactly how much she costs.

Lily's commodity psychology also figures strongly in her problematic relationships with men. Because she can't afford to keep herself in the style required if she is to socialize with the Trenors and the Dorsets, her goal is to marry a wealthy man from this group and thereby perma-

nently fix her position among them. While "a few years ago it had suf-
ficed her" to take "her daily meed of pleasure" from "the luxury of others," as the novel opens, "she was beginning to chafe at the obligations
it imposed, to feel herself a mere pensioner on the splendour" of her
friends (27; bk. 1, ch. 3). Therefore, she sets her sights on the eligible heir
to the Gryce fortune, Percy Gryce. However, once she is certain that a
proposal of marriage is forthcoming, Lily loses her advantage by
spending the day with Lawrence Selden instead of with Gryce, as
planned. Because her attention to Selden interferes with Bertha Dorset's
amorous plans for that young man, Bertha revenges herself, as Lily was
warned she would, by scaring off Gryce with stories about Lily's husband hunting and gambling debts. Lily thus ruins her chances with
Gryce just as she has ruined her chances with every eligible man who
has wanted to marry her over the past eleven years.

Lily's apparent lapse in strategy with Percy Gryce is not, as Irving
Howe claims, the result of spontaneous behavior (121) or, as Wendy
Gimbel would have it, one of her miscalculations (44). The pattern of
Lily's behavior is too consistent to ascribe it to impulse or miscalcula-
tion. As the protagonist's friend Carry Fisher observes, the same thing
happens every time Lily is about to receive a proposal of marriage: "She
works like a slave preparing the ground and sowing her seed; but the
day she ought to be reaping the harvest she over-sleeps herself or goes
off on a picnic" (197; bk. 2, ch. 1). Mrs. Fisher guesses correctly that Lily
ruins her chances of marriage deliberately, but her speculation that she
does so "because, at heart, she despises the things she's trying for" (197;
bk. 2, ch. 1) is only partially correct. What Lily despises is not "her pre-
determined role as object" (Wershoven 58) or the idea of herself as a
commodity (Fryer 86): as we have seen, her goal has long been to be the
best object on the market, and she takes great pleasure in the signs of
her success. Rather, Lily is unconsciously repelled by the psychosexual
demands of an intimate relationship.

Lily's self-image as art object reflects and supports a psychological
structure that is at odds with the psychosexual requirements of marriage. Objets d'art are commodities that are seen but not touched, and
Lily's desire to be an art object reflects her desire to be admired from
afar, to be viewed without being touched. Like a framed portrait or the
hard surfaces of the finely crafted jewelry she loves, Lily wants to be beyond history—impervious to the "humiliating contingencies" of life
(191; bk. 1, ch. 8)—and beyond the existential inwardness that an

awareness of existential contingency promotes: "more completely than any other expression of wealth," jewels enhanced by an artistic setting "symbolized the life she longed to lead, the life of fastidious aloofness and refinement" (94; bk. 1, ch. 8). Physical intimacy endangers the transcendental project because it touches nerve endings tied to emotions (fear, anger, love, hate) and moods (anxiety, insecurity) that preclude the possibility of achieving transcendence. As Walter Davis observes, when transcendence becomes a major project, sexuality becomes a major threat (*Inwardness and Existence* 82).[7]

Lily's desire to aestheticize herself out of existence informs her life so pervasively that we see its expression even in the seal with which she secures her letters: "a grey seal with *Beyond!* beneath a flying ship" (163; bk. 1, ch. 14). And it is this same desire we see in her reaction to her stay with Mrs. Norma Hatch, her first sojourn into the twilight area beyond the Sam Gormer periphery of the Trenor-Dorset beau monde: "Lily had an odd sense of being behind the social tapestry, on the side where the threads were knotted and the loose ends hung" (290; bk. 2, ch. 9). She prefers the world of formal manners, where familiarity is kept at a minimum and where the right side of the tapestry is gazed upon by an admiring throng who always remain at a safe distance.

Lily's desire not to be touched is particularly apparent, of course, in her interpersonal relationships. While her avoidance of physical contact with unappealing, predatory men like Gus Trenor, George Dorset, and Simon Rosedale certainly needs no explanation, Lily doesn't like being touched even by her attractive women friends, as we see when she "extricate[s] herself" from Judy Trenor's embrace during a conversation between the two women at Bellomont (47; bk. 1, ch. 4) and "dr[aws] back" from Carry Fisher's "clasp" after the reading of Mrs. Peniston's will (242; bk. 2, ch. 5). As Gerty Farish knows, "Lily disliked to be caressed," and therefore Gerty "had long ago learned to check her demonstrative impulses toward her friend" (176; bk. 1, ch. 14). It is a joke that has the ring of truth when Lily facetiously says to Carry Fisher, "Other things being equal, I think I should prefer a half-husband" (249; bk. 2, ch. 5). While the reason for her unwillingness to marry a rigid, boring fool like Percy Gryce is no mystery, the Italian prince she lost in a similar manner (197; bk. 2, ch. 1), her rejection of Lord Hubert's suit (209; bk. 2, ch. 2), and the "few good chances" Lily confesses to having lost when she "first came out" (10; bk. 1, ch.1) reveal that her distaste for potential husbands is not limited to a single type.

Although she does seem, at one point, to resign herself to marriage with Rosedale, it is noteworthy that she actively pursues him only when she has reason to believe that he doesn't want to marry her anymore (251–52; bk. 2, ch. 5) and, even more significantly, only when it serves as a strategy to save her from marrying George Dorset (259–60; bk. 2, ch. 6). Using "another man" to deflect her attention from and ruin her chances with a potential husband is the same technique Lily used when she avoided marrying the Italian prince by paying too much attention to his stepson (197; bk. 2, ch. 1) and, as we have seen, when she avoids a proposal from Percy Gryce by paying too much attention to Selden (56; bk. 1, ch. 5). This technique both keeps her from having to marry and sets up a smoke screen that protects her from probing too deeply the motives behind her behavior.

Given Lily's desire to avoid intimacy, how can her attraction to Lawrence Selden be explained? Although, at first glance, her relationship with this character may seem to contradict the assertion that Lily dislikes physical contact, Selden's appeal can be seen as a direct outgrowth of her role as art object and the desire for emotional insulation it represents. For Selden shares Lily's desire to aestheticize her body, which is part of the larger project he shares with her: the desire to escape existential inwardness. In order to understand the psychological dynamics of his project and how it is related to Lily's, it is necessary to consider the relationship among woman's body, the commodity, the art object, and the fetish, or the (p)art object.

To begin, we must examine the way in which Lily is an object for Selden. Just as the Trenor-Dorset clique appreciates Lily's uniqueness as a commodity in a way that the Gormers do not, Lawrence Selden appreciates her as an art object in a way that the Trenor-Dorset group does not. As Cynthia Griffin Wolff aptly observes, the relationship between Selden and Lily is one between connoisseur and collectible: for him, Lily is an idealized object that the actual woman can never match (129–30). However, the standard of perfection that Selden demands she become is not "a flawless, absolutely constant embodiment of [moral] virtue" (129), as Wolff suggests, but an absolutely constant embodiment of aesthetic perfection. For it is only as the perfect aesthetic object that Lily can help Selden fulfill his own transcendental project.

Selden's clearest statement of his transcendental project occurs in the oft-quoted "republic of the spirit" speech. Here he explains to Lily that his idea of success is the attainment of "personal freedom," freedom "from everything—from money, from poverty, from ease and anxiety, from all the material accidents. To keep a kind of republic of the spirit— that's what I call success" (71; bk. 1, ch. 6). While Wolff (129) and Howe (120) believe that this speech refers to Selden's moral vision, this character's attempt to achieve a "republic of the spirit" has, instead, all the earmarks of an idealized aesthetic quest.

Raised in a household where limited funds and refined taste put a premium on the few fine things the family could afford—good books, fine paintings, old lace—Selden never lost the appreciation for aesthetic quality he learned as a boy, an appreciation that was never marred by the kind of material overindulgence practiced by his wealthier acquaintances (160–61; bk. 1, ch. 14). As a result of this early training, Selden has a "responsive fancy" that gives him "magic glimpses of the boundary world between fact and imagination," and "he could yield to vision-making influences as completely as a child to the spell of a fairy-tale" (140–41; bk. 1, ch. 12). This ability, coupled with his desire to be free from the exigencies of a world in which his moderate income affords him little protection from "material accidents," is responsible for his pursuit of a spiritual republic to compensate for the inequities of the concrete world in which he finds himself. Of course, Selden's quest for transcendence is a quest for a form of social superiority as well: Selden wants to be "above" his social group in every sense of *above*. The irony is that this very desire, because it is socially produced, ties him to the society he would transcend. Selden doesn't escape social desire; he merely abstracts it.

Lily represents for Selden the romantic incarnation of his aesthetic values. He was bred to have "the stoic's carelessness of material things, combined with the Epicurean's pleasure in them," and "nowhere was the blending of the two ingredients so essential as in the character of a pretty woman" (161; bk. 1, ch. 14). When Selden believes that the Lily Bart he sees in the tableau vivant is "the real Lily," it is because she "is one with . . . her image" (143; bk. 1, ch. 12). This is the Lily—the external sign of beauty, the perfect object—with whom Selden finally admits he is smitten and for whom he "luxuriate[s] . . . in the sense of [his] complete surrender" (143; bk. 1, ch. 12). And just as it is an aesthetic ideal that attracts Selden to Lily, it is her inevitable violation of this ideal that repulses him. As Davis observes,

> Idealization necessarily pictures the other in terms of external signs— money, beauty, virginity, etc.—because the other can have no qualities suggesting interiority or otherness. The perfect object is one who has achieved successful externalization and is one with his or her image. But this is also where the whole project begins to unravel. For such a one is open to endless appropriation by others. . . . (*Inwardness and Existence* 309)

Thus, each time Selden rejects Lily—for example, after seeing her emerge alone from Gus Trenor's house late at night, after learning that she joined the Duchess of Beltshire's loose crowd instead of heading home after the *Sabrina* incident, after seeing her apparent resolve to remain in the employ of Mrs. Hatch—it is not because, as many critics believe,[8] she has violated his social or moral prejudices but because she has violated his aesthetic ideal. It is not, as Frances L. Restuccia argues, a "perfectly virtuous object" that Selden seeks in Lily (230) but a perfect aesthetic object. Each time Lily sacrifices the "republic of the spirit" for material comforts, she devalues Selden's private, romantic world of beauty—the only world he can offer her—in favor of the crass public world of people like Bertha Dorset and the Duchess of Beltshire:[9]

> His real detachment from her had taken place, not at the lurid moment of disenchantment, but now, in the sober after-light of discrimination, where he saw her definitely divided from him by the crudeness of a choice which seemed to deny the very differences he felt in her. It was before him again in its completeness—the choice in which she was content to rest: in the stupid costliness of the food and the showy dullness of the talk, in the freedom of speech which never arrived at wit and the freedom of act which never made for romance. (200; bk. 2, ch. 1)

And, significantly, Selden perceives Lily's failure to live up to his "republic of the spirit" in terms of the change in her as an aesthetic object. When, for example, he meets her for the first time since the night he saw her leaving Trenor's house, Selden notices that

> a subtle change had passed over the quality of her beauty. Then [during their brief interlude in the Bry's conservatory after the tableaux vivants] it had had a transparency through which the fluctuations of the spirit were sometimes tragically visible; now its impenetrable surface sug-

gested a process of crystallization which had fused her whole being into one hard brilliant substance. The change had struck Mrs. Fisher as a rejuvenation: to Selden it seemed like that moment of pause and arrest when the warm fluidity of youth is chilled into its final shape. (199–200; bk. 2, ch. 1)

Although the apparent loss of "fluctuations of the spirit" may have moral implications for the protagonist, Selden nevertheless focuses on the aesthetic domain, on the result of Lily's change as it manifests itself in her beauty. The concern here is not ethical but aesthetic, romantic, transcendental.

At first glance, Selden's aestheticization of Lily contrasts sharply with the rather crass commodification of this young woman by the Trenor-Dorset group. As Carol Wershoven notes (50), during the tableaux vivants, in contrast with the rest of the company, who focus on the scantiness of Lily's drapery and speculate on her intention to display her form (for social profit, of course), Selden is moved by the "eternal harmony of which her beauty was a part," and he angrily condemns a society unable to appreciate the virtues of her loveliness (142; bk. 1, ch. 12). However, his aestheticization of Lily intersects with the other characters' commodification of her in a way that is central to the psychology involved: in both commodification and aestheticization, the object becomes a fetish.

According to Marx, as soon as an object becomes a commodity, "it is changed into something transcendent" (26). Just as "the productions of the human brain appear [in the religious experience] as independent beings endowed with life and entering into relation both with one another and the human race. . . . so it is in the world of commodities with the products of [human] hands" (Marx 27). While the religious fetish is endowed with life in the form of metaphysical meaning, the commodity, Marx explains, is endowed with life in the form of social meaning (27). However, in both cases that meaning exists in a realm beyond the actual physical properties of the object in question. And because it "stands for" something beyond itself, the commodity can also function as a partial object; that is, the commodity can be a fetish in the Freudian sense as well: it can be used as a substitute point of focus in order to mask and deny a painful psychological reality.

Lily's body, as aestheticized by Selden as well as by herself, has the qualities of a fetish in both these ways. The "eternal harmony" (142; bk. 1, ch. 12) of her "jewel-like" beauty (94; bk. 1, ch. 8), for which Lily strives and which only Selden appreciates, is a meaning that points to a realm beyond the actual physical properties of her flesh-and-blood body. And her aestheticized body is also a surrogate. Selden's focus on Lily as objet d'art masks and denies the same painful psychological reality that Lily's self-aestheticization seeks to mask and deny: psychological vulnerability to existential contingency, a vulnerability that increases in direct proportion to one's poverty and that promotes an existential inwardness neither character desires. Thus, Lily and Selden's mutual attraction is grounded in a shared transcendental project. Selden fetishizes Lily's aestheticized body as a sign of the transcendence, of the escape from existential inwardness, he seeks. And Lily, in order to achieve the aestheticized body—the self-reification—she desires, fetishizes Selden's gaze.

Because Lily sees Selden as a connoisseur of objets d'art, his appreciation of her beauty is extremely important. When she receives a note from him the morning after her stunning success in the tableaux vivants, "the sight of Selden's writing brought back the culminating moment of her triumph: the moment when she had read in his eyes that no philosophy was proof against her power. It would be pleasant to have that sensation again . . . no one else could give it to her in its fulness" (147; bk. 1, ch. 13). This mutual gaze, which recurs throughout the novel, underscores Lily and Selden's narcissistic folie à deux. As Joan Rivière explains in her 1929 article, "Womanliness as Masquerade," women, as objects, look only in order to be looked at while looking. Lily likes to watch Selden watch her because it is his gaze that fixes her as the aesthetic object she wants to be. Conversely, her return gaze, as aesthetic object, fixes Selden in his desired identity as connoisseur. The pair thus fulfills the desire of each for self-reification, for self-abstraction.

As an abstraction, Selden's attractiveness to Lily lies largely in the ways in which he is beyond her reach. Lily's desire to feel her aesthetic power over Selden is therefore increased by the uncertainty that she will always be able to do so. When they meet at the Van Osburgh wedding, for example, Lily expects him to be still under the sway of their last encounter at Bellomont, where he first revealed a personal interest in her. She is distressed to see that now

> there was not the least trace of embarrassment in his voice, and as he
> spoke, leaning slightly against the jamb of the window, and letting his
> eyes rest on her in the frank enjoyment of her grace, she felt with a faint

chill of regret that he had gone back without an effort to the footing on which they had stood before their last talk together. (99; bk. 1, ch. 8)

This experience is unique for Lily: she is accustomed to easy victories in her sentimental experiments. Finding Selden frequently beyond her reach makes him all the more attractive to her, not because she wants what she can't have, but because his unavailability protects her from an intimacy that, unconsciously, she doesn't really desire.

Similarly, Selden seems deliciously beyond Lily's reach because of the transcendental project—the "republic of the spirit"—he represents, which resonates powerfully with the otherworldly, romantic quality we see in her girlhood idea of a perfect husband: "Lily's preference would have been for an English nobleman with political ambitions and vast estates; or . . . an Italian prince with a castle in the Apennines and an hereditary office in the Vatican" (36–37; bk. 1, ch. 3). Even Lily's perception of Selden's manner and physical features places him in another world:

His reputed cultivation was generally regarded as a slight obstacle to easy intercourse, but Lily . . . was attracted by this attribute, which she felt would have had its distinction in an *older society*. It was, moreover, one of his gifts to look his part; to have a height which lifted his head above the crowd, and keenly-modelled dark features which, in a land of amorphous types, gave him the air of belonging to a *more specialized race*, of carrying the impress of a *concentrated past*. Expansive persons found him a little dry . . . but this air of friendly aloofness . . . was the quality which piqued Lily's interest. Everything about him accorded with the *fastidious* element in her taste. (68; bk. 1, ch. 60, my emphasis)

It is clear in this passage that Selden appeals to Lily because of her girlhood desire for men who don't exist in the material world, a desire for the otherworldly that she has carried with her into adulthood. Indeed, we learn that when she had the opportunity to marry a flesh-and-blood English nobleman or a real Italian prince, she threw it away.

Although Lily and Selden do make physical contact on one occasion—they kiss—the context in which the event occurs reveals that it is not the manifestation of a budding sexual inclination on Lily's part. Following the tableaux vivants—which clearly gave both characters the feeling that they were, for the moment, in another, more romantic world beyond existential reality—the pair enjoy a quiet tête à tête in the conservatory, in a scene whose otherworldly, transcendental elements are foregrounded: "The magic place was deserted: there was no sound but the plash of the water on the lily-pads," and the "drift of music" from the nearby house seems as if it "might have been blown across a sleeping lake. . . . Selden and Lily stood still, accepting the unreality of the scene as part of their own dream-like sensations" (144; bk. 1, ch. 12). Then, as they sit in quiet conversation,

> her face turned to him with the soft motion of a flower. His own met it slowly, and their lips touched.
>
> She drew back and rose from her seat. Selden rose too, and they stood facing each other. Suddenly she caught his hand and pressed it a moment against her cheek.
>
> "Ah, love me, love me—but don't tell me so!" she sighed with her eyes in his; and before he could speak she had turned and slipped through the arch of boughs, disappearing in the brightness of the room beyond. (145; bk. 1, ch. 12)

The sentimental novels of Emma Bovary's girlhood could hardly have produced a better line than "Ah, love me, love me—but don't tell me so!" Both the semantic content of the phrase and the manner in which it's delivered bespeak the subtext of Lily's behavior in this scene: what she is really saying is "love me, but don't do anything to which I will have to respond in the real world." Indeed, the next morning Lily refers to the "scene in the Brys' conservatory" as "a part of her dreams," and she feels "annoyance" at Selden for sending her a note requesting a visit so soon afterward: "She had not expected to awake to such evidence of [the previous night's] reality. . . . It was so unlike [Selden] to yield to such an irrational impulse!" (147; bk. 1, ch. 13).

For Wendy Gimbel (56) and Diana Trilling (112–14), who believe that a good deal of Lily's behavior is motivated by her love for Selden, the protagonist's "love me—but don't tell me so!" could refer to the conflict between her desire to marry him and her need for the kind of wealth he cannot supply. On the contrary, Lily's conflict, up to this point, has been between her desire for wealth and her desire to avoid marriage to the rich men who could provide it. In Selden she has, for the first time, an unconflicted romantic relationship: she can share her desire for the otherworldly, and play out all of its romantic possibilities, without having to face the importunities of a man whose station in life allows him to press his suit.

That Lily and Selden's aestheticization of her body supports the same desire served by commodification is also illustrated in the pair's use of economic metaphors during their first conversation in the novel. Here the couple discuss the social conventions regarding women of New York's upper crust. Lily tells Selden,

> "Your coat's a little shabby—but who cares? It doesn't keep people from asking you to dine. If I were shabby no one would have me: a woman is asked out as much for her clothes as for herself. The clothes are the background, the frame, if you like: they don't make success, but they are a part of it. Who wants a dingy woman? We are expected to be pretty and well-dressed till we drop—and if we can't keep it up alone, we have to go into partnership."
>
> Selden glanced at her with amusement: it was impossible, even with her lovely eyes imploring him, to take a sentimental view of her case.
>
> "Ah, well, there must be plenty of capital on the look-out for such an investment. Perhaps you'll meet your fate tonight. . . . " (12; bk. 1, ch. 1)

Of course, Lily and Selden's use of economic metaphors in this passage underscores the profit-and-loss nature of what Lily calls the "business" of achieving social success. If a woman hasn't the financial means to keep herself socially marketable, she must acquire a husband for the same reason a businessman often acquires a partner: to maintain her exchange value by maintaining her capital worth. However, their language has another, more powerful effect: it distances Lily and Selden from the objects of their discourse. Lily's real project in discussing woman as commodity in this excerpt is to distance herself emotionally from the horror of her own situation as a genteel woman of scant means trying to maintain her social position among the very wealthy. Similarly, Selden's real project is to avoid getting in touch with his own romantic feelings for Lily. As long as he can view her problem as a question of goods and exchange, and remain amused by it, he won't be touched by the pathos of her plight, and he won't have to deal with his attraction to her. Thus, the couple's use of economic metaphors, when we first see them together, creates a language of abstraction that both mirrors and foreshadows the transcendental project they will share in the second half of the novel.

Lily's attraction to Selden's otherworldliness, and her attempt to belong to the romantic world she glimpses through his eyes, also help explain the moral dimension that, as we have seen, so many critics associate with the protagonist's ultimate preference for Selden's approval over that of the Trenor-Dorset clan.[10] Even Cynthia Griffin

Wolff, who recognizes that Selden desires Lily for her aesthetic qualities and therefore confuses the real woman with the ideal (126), believes
that both characters are attracted to the notion of a "republic of the
spirit" for its moral dimension (129). While I agree with Blake Nevius
that the *possibility* of a moral dimension in Lily occurs at the novel's
close, the critical focus on her ethics overlooks the psychology that informs them. For example, her desire to discharge her debt to Trenor, although initially born of her desire to reestablish her relationship with
his wife, Judy (239; bk. 2, ch. 4), soon becomes symbolic behavior, not in
the literary sense, but in the psychological. This debt—like her disastrous voyage on the *Sabrina* and her acquisition of Bertha Dorset's letters to Selden—represents one of Lily's most horrifying experiences of
existential contingency and the existential inwardness that accompanies it; in closing the door on this chapter of her life, she wants to close
the door on existential experience. The hypermorality she develops
during the novel's closing chapters, which comes to a head in her destruction of Bertha's letters, is a function of her desire to rise above the
Trenor-Dorset group in the way she believes Selden has risen above it:
by transcending the existential inwardness that keeps him aware of his
vulnerability to life's uncertainties. Lily wants to be admitted to
Selden's romantic "republic of the spirit," and she knows only one way
to get what she wants: by becoming the perfect object for her audience.

As Wolff observes, Lily "has learned so thoroughly to experience
herself as an object that is being observed by others—not directly as an
integrated human being—that her sense of 'self' is confirmed only
when she elicits reactions from others" (128). Therefore, the protagonist
must do whatever she thinks a member of the "republic of the spirit"
would do in any given situation. At this point, hers is an outerdirected
"morality"; because she hasn't internalized the principles upon which it
operates, her moral perceptions tend to apprehend issues in black-and-
white terms, as the moral perceptions of young children often do.[11] This
is why she cannot save herself by letting Bertha Dorset know she has
possession of her incriminating letters to Lawrence Selden. Although
no third party would ever see them—and Selden could, therefore, in no
way be hurt by them—the letters are written, as Rosedale says when he
realizes the connection, "to *him* [Selden]" (273; bk. 2, ch. 7). Lily thus relinquishes her last means of regaining her social position and, with it,

her last means of avoiding the fatal dose of chloral that inevitably follows her growing dependence on the sleeping drug.

Because most critical analyses of Lily Bart are informed by the victim model of the relationship between the individual and the socius, most view her death as a severe criticism of the culture that both produced and destroyed her. However, a dialectical model of subjectivity suggests that the protagonist's death has another function as well: to complete and safeguard Lily and Selden's shared transcendental project. During the novel's final four chapters—which take us from Lily's last days at Madame Regina's millinery workshop to her fatal overdose— we see a different Lily Bart, capable of a great deal of human warmth and with a new capacity to make real contact with others. For example, she responds with "the first sincere words she had ever spoken to him" (309; bk. 2, ch. 10) to Rosedale's brave offer to visit her after she is dismissed from the milliner's and is living in poverty in a run-down neighborhood. Similarly, she frankly confesses to Selden his importance in her life without expecting or requiring a response in kind: "She had passed beyond the phase of well-bred reciprocity, in which every demonstration must be scrupulously proportioned to the emotion it elicits, and generosity of feeling is the only ostentation condemned" (323; bk. 2, ch. 12). Even her distaste for physical closeness is suspended when, during a visit with Nettie Struther, she picks up that young woman's child and "felt the soft weight sink trustfully against her breast . . . thrill[ing] her with a sense of warmth" (333; bk. 2, ch. 13).

This is not the Lily Bart who commodified herself and others; however, neither is this the heroic figure who, through loss and suffering, has developed into the superior moral being many critics want to see in her. Rather, this is a dying woman who is taking her leave of this world. She need not fear the existential inwardness to which her emotions will make her liable only because she will soon be forever beyond it. What we have here is a commodity fetish for which death can be the only issue, the only completion of its transcendental project. Lily herself becomes briefly aware of the relationship between death and the avoidance of existential inwardness—though, of course, she doesn't recognize it as such—upon returning home after her final, exhilarating visit to Selden. She has just received the check for her inheritance:

There was the cheque in her desk, for instance—she meant to use it in paying her debt to Trenor; but she foresaw that when the money came she would put off doing so. . . . The thought terrified her—she dreaded to fall from the height of her last moment with Lawrence Selden. . . . She felt an intense longing to prolong, to perpetuate, the momentary exaltation of her spirit. If only life could end now. . . . (338; bk. 2, ch. 13)

Furthermore, if we regard death as a psychological force—as Freud does in *Beyond the Pleasure Principle*—rather than merely as a biological event, then its presence in Lily's consciousness before her biological death can guide us in understanding the nature and significance of that event.

Death makes its first, and perhaps most direct, appearance in the form of the sleeping drug upon which Lily has grown dependent. The protagonist's "dread" of "having to pass the chemist's" on her way home from work, the chemist's ominous warning that "a drop or two more [beyond the prescribed dosage] and off you go," Lily's agony of apprehension lest he should refuse her the drug, the way "the mere touch of the packet thrilled her tired nerves" (303; bk. 2, ch. 10)—all these elements suggest that we are in the presence of death. Lily's physical aspect reinforces this feeling. Selden notices "the pallour of her delicately-hollowed face" (322; bk. 2, ch. 12), and "he saw too, under the loose lines of her dress, how the curves of her figure had shrunk to angularity . . . how the red play of the flame sharpened her nostrils, and intensified the blackness of the shadows which struck up from her cheekbones to her eyes" (326; bk. 2, ch. 12). This language could easily be used to describe a corpse. It is no wonder that Selden has "a strange sense of foreboding" or that the pair "looked at each other with a kind of solemnity, as though they stood in the presence of death" (326; bk. 2, ch. 12).

As these passages indicate, Lily is inhabited by death well before she actually dies, a condition that suggests that her desire for the transcendental—for the Unchanging, for substance—is becoming irresistible. Although Lily doesn't commit suicide in the deliberate and premeditated way this term usually implies,[12] she so desires the "brief bath of oblivion" the drug gives her (339; bk. 2, ch. 13) that she deliberately refrains from considering the risk she is taking when she increases the dose to compensate for her growing immunity to its soporific effect: "She did not, in truth, consider the question very closely—the physical craving for sleep was her only sustained sensation. Her mind shrank from the glare of thought as instinctively as eyes contract in a blaze of light—darkness, darkness was what she must have at any cost" (340; bk. 2, ch. 13). Lily's has to be a passive suicide because only an "accidental" death allows her to preserve the illusion she wants to preserve: that she hasn't acted, hasn't chosen, but has remained an object to the end.

Particularly striking in this context, the language used to describe Lily's feelings when she takes the drug reveals that the chloral is more than a simple haven from the misery of her waking life: she is enamored of its deathlike effect.

> She lay very still, waiting with a sensuous pleasure for the first effects of the soporific. She knew in advance what form they would take—the gradual cessation of the inner throb, the soft approach of passiveness, as though an invisible hand made magic passes over her in the darkness. The very slowness and hesitancy of the effect increased its fascination: it was delicious to lean over and look down into the dim abysses of unconsciousness. (340; bk. 2, ch. 13)

The unconsciousness the drug brings her is as "delicious" to Lily now, and as sensuously described, as her luxurious breakfast in bed at Bellomont and her morning-after reminiscence of her conquest of Selden in the Brys' conservatory. Death—or deathlike unconsciousness—is as attractive to her now as those experiences were then because it is the only sphere of the otherworldly that remains open to her. She can no longer reify herself as a commodity for the Trenor-Dorset clique because they are no longer buying what she has to sell. And she feels she can no longer hope to share Selden's otherworldly domain, the only alternative to her former life-style—however vaguely conceived—she has ever been able to imagine, because, having failed for so long to live up to his romantic ideal, her efforts to live up to it at the end of the novel seem to produce little change in his behavior toward her. Thus, "she saw herself forever shut out from [his] inmost self" (323; bk. 2, ch. 12). Feeling herself alone and helpless, she lets herself die. As Freud explains, "When the ego finds itself in an excessive real danger which it believes itself unable to overcome by its own strength, it . . . sees itself deserted by all protecting forces and lets itself die" ("The Ego and the Id" 58). While there may have been other "protecting forces" available to Lily—her budding friendship with Rosedale and Gerty Farish's unflagging moral support—they wouldn't have protected her in the way she most desired: from the existential inwardness produced by her vulnerability to the physical realities of life on the "wrong side" of the "social tapestry." Only the Trenor-Dorset life-style or Selden's other-worldly vision, Lily believes, could have that protection, and now only death can provide it.

For Selden as well, Lily's death is the only real source of the abstract perfection he seeks in her. It is no coincidence that Selden is finally able to tell Lily he loves her, is finally drawn "penitent and reconciled to her side," only when she is dead: "He knelt by the bed and bent over her, draining their last moment to its lees; and in the silence there passed between them the word which made all clear" (347; bk. 2, ch. 14). These closing lines are as deliciously romantic as the description we saw earlier of Lily's relaxation into a luxurious sleep after taking the fatal dose of chloral. Her death is thus the consummation of both characters' desire for abstract perfection, and it fulfills the unconscious psychological agenda that has operated for Lily since she first came to rely on Selden's otherworldly vision for her refuge, since she first found "the thought of confiding in him . . . as seductive as the river's flow to the suicide" (183; bk. 1, ch. 15).

Unlike Flaubert, who dramatizes every nuance of Emma Bovary's slow demise, thereby metaphorically underscoring the nature of that character's self-unraveling, Wharton accomplishes Lily's death behind closed doors. It is appropriate that the author thus undercuts the concrete, biological reality of her protagonist's death, not only because we need to focus instead on the social implications of Lily's decease, but because it is as an abstraction and a mystification—and as the desire for self-abstraction and self-mystification—that Lily's death provides the appropriate closure for her life. The closest she comes to embracing psychological possibility is by embracing, in her imagination, its representative: Nettie Struther's child. Given that this embrace occurs only in her mind, and that this representative of psychological possibility is a member both of an oppressed gender and of an oppressed class, the chances that such possibility will be realized in Wharton's commodified world are rather slim.

The dialectical reading of the protagonist I have offered is not intended to let the socius off the hook but to put the individual on it as well. My explanation of Lily's behavior throughout the novel as the function of her role as aesthetic commodity fetish attempts to reveal the psychological characteristics of the protagonist's ideological investments in order to explain, in part, why she makes such investments and why she sacrifices so much in their name. In the society Wharton describes in *The House of Mirth*—a society whose values thrive in America today in our own ubiquitous marketplace culture—woman forgoes psychological possibility as the price paid to escape existential inwardness. And commodity psychology, which is tied to the American dream's merger of the economic and spiritual dimensions of human experience, offers the means to this end.

Clearly, the significance of Lily Bart's death, like the significance of her life, cannot be explained by her attraction to one side or the other of a moral opposition between the Trenor-Dorset milieu and the spiritual realm she associates with Lawrence Selden, for it is the opportunity they offer for self-reification that attracts her to both. While the protagonist's intelligence, sensitivity, and delicacy make her far superior to—and infinitely more sympathetic than—her milieu, the view that she is victimized by her social stratum for being too moral to survive in it casts her in terms that are too simple to reflect the depth and complexity of Wharton's characterization. If, in Lily's world as in our own, commodity culture claims many victims, *The House of Mirth* reveals that one powerful reason why can be found in the nature of the psychological payoffs it offers. It is not enough, then or now, to say simply that commodity culture victimizes women, for such a formulation of the problem leaves women's individual strength and collective power out of the equation. How does commodity culture lead women into collusion with their own victimization? This is the question we must also ask, and it is a question *The House of Mirth* can help us answer.

2

The Romance of the Commodity

The Cancellation of Identity in F. Scott Fitzgerald's *Great Gatsby*

If *The House of Mirth* reveals the insidious nature of the American dream's commodified ideology, *The Great Gatsby* (1925) has served to underscore our blindness to it. Perhaps more than any other work of American literature, F. Scott Fitzgerald's best-known novel has elicited a critical response that reveals Americans' desire to sustain their nostalgia for an idealized America—and an idealized American ideology—as an absolute positive value of pristine origin. What Marius Bewley said of Jay Gatsby in 1954 has long represented the feeling of a good many readers: Gatsby is "the energy of the spirit's resistance" and "immunity to the final contamination" of "cheapness and vulgarity" (13); he is "an heroic personification of the American romantic hero, the true heir of the American dream" (14). As Charles C. Nash puts it, "Emerson's 'Infinitude of the Private Man'" is "best represented by Jay Gatsby, for whom all things are possible" (23). Gatsby is thus seen as "a sensual saint" (Dillon 50) whose "dream . . . enobles him (Cartwright 229), "a representative American hero . . . though of course not average" (Hart 34). Even when the protagonist's darker side is acknowledged, it is excused: "Gatsby can be both criminal and romantic hero because the book creates for him a visionary moral standard that transcends the conventional and that his life affirms" (Cartwright 232).[1] For these readers, the American dream, like the character of Gatsby with whom it is identified, represents something pure and true—a "sacred energy" (Dillon 61)—that has been corrupted over time by the influence of the moral wasteland that continues to extend its borders farther into the core of American society. The corruption, they believe, lies not in the American dream or in Jay Gatsby but in what surrounds and victimizes the protagonist: Wolfsheim's exploitativeness, Daisy's duplicity, Tom's treachery, and the shallowness of an American populace—represented by Gatsby's parasitical party guests—whose moral fiber has declined with each passing year.

The Great Gatsby's title character, however—far from being, as Bewley puts it, Tom's "opposite number" (24), "all aspiration and goodness" (25)—is the Buchanans' mirror image.[2] Tom, Daisy, and Gatsby all reveal the psychological politics of the American dream's commodification of identity. As we shall see, Tom and Daisy reveal the psychology of the commodity as it is manifest in gender-specific cultural roles: Tom personifies commodity culture as the subject of desire, and Daisy personifies commodity culture as the object of desire. Gatsby does not stand in opposition to the Buchanans' relationship to commodity culture; rather, he is its abstraction, a distinction that has been missed by the victim model of subjectivity informing most analyses of the protagonist. That is, to understand Jay Gatsby, we must understand Tom and Daisy Buchanan as the concrete manifestations of the culture that, in its abstract form, constitutes Gatsby's desire to cancel his own identity, to obliterate his past, as a means of avoiding the existential inwardness that accompanies the experience of lack, loss, or limitation.

Thus, this chapter will argue that The Great Gatsby does not portray the American dream as an absolute positive value of pristine origin that somehow gets corrupted. Rather, because it is a commodity—in this case, a sign invested with the desire for consumption as the principal mode of production—the American dream is itself a source of corruption. Gatsby's emotional investment in this dream does not indicate that he is somehow immune to contamination but that he is its representative. And I will suggest that readers who judge Gatsby to be of finer stuff than the world surrounding him might do so, in part, from a desire to protect their ideological investment in an American dream of their own. Finally, I will examine an important strand of the narrative that operates as a powerful countermovement against the novel's insights into commodity psychology: the seductive appeal with which the commodity is portrayed in this text, an appeal that is behind much of Jay Gatsby's emotional seduction of narrator Nick Carraway and of the many readers who rally to his cause.

As Edwin Fussell notes, the underlying assumption in The Great Gatsby is "that all the magic of the world can be had for money" (44), and as the novel reveals, it is the paradoxical "meeting" of these two terms—

money and *magic*—that defines the American dream. Nowhere in the novel is the magical power of money more efficiently and successfully exploited than by Tom Buchanan. He does not, as Roger Lewis claims, understand "that polo ponies or cufflinks are all he is buying" (51); he has learned how to buy social status and self-image as well. He is a perfect representative of pure agency: a subjectivity for whom all else must be object, and for a rich man who relates to the world through his money, all objects are commodities.

Tom's marriage to Daisy Fay was clearly an exchange of Daisy's youth, beauty, and social standing for Tom's money and power and the image of strength and stability they imparted to him. Appropriately, the symbol of this "purchase" was the $350,000 string of pearls Tom gave his bride-to-be. Jordan's reference to the necklace, during her account of Daisy's wedding, defines it in terms of the purchase—and the oppression—it represents, especially as we see Daisy wearing the pearls for the first time right after her failed attempt to call off the marriage. The diction of Jordan's portrait of Daisy at this moment—"When we walked out of the room, the pearls were around her neck and the incident was over" (77–78; ch. 4)—subtly emphasizes Daisy's submission: the pearls, not Daisy, are the subject of the sentence, and they are "around her neck," a phrase easily associated with a slave collar or a noose. Similarly, Tom uses his money and social rank to "purchase" Myrtle Wilson and the numerous other working-class women with whom he has affairs, such as the chambermaid with whom he was involved three months after his marriage to Daisy and the "common but pretty" (107; ch. 6) young woman he picks up at Gatsby's party.

Of course, Tom's commodity psychology is not limited to his relationships with women. Much of Buchanan's pleasure in his expensive possessions is a function of their sign-exchange value, of the social status their ownership confers on him. Social status is important to him not just to impress others but to impress himself as well. Like Sartre's Julien Fleurier, Tom's sense of his own identity is largely a product of how he believes others see him. His desire to impress others is great because his desire to impress himself is great. "I've got a nice place here" (7; ch. 1), he tells Nick, but he is saying it to himself as well. In this context, his house's "pedigree" is an important detail: "It belonged to Demaine, the oil man," he points out (8; ch. 1), as if the house's "pedigree" could confer a pedigree on him.

Why should a man like Tom—rich, good-looking, physically

strong—need to impress himself? One reason is provided by Nick: Tom "had been one of the most powerful ends that ever played football at New Haven—a national figure in a way, one of those men who reach such an acute limited excellence at twenty-one that everything afterward savors of anticlimax" (6; ch. 1). The view that Tom is trying to recapture past glory is supported by his seductions of women exclusively from the working class. With women of a lower socioeconomic standing than his, he can be the hero they've been hoping would rescue them from the limitations placed upon them by their class. Certainly, this is the role in which Myrtle Wilson casts him, as we see when she tries to play the part of the society hostess at the apartment Tom keeps for their rendezvous (29–32; ch. 2). In this way, he can experience a facsimile of the kind of attention, the feeling of power, the ego gratification, he must have experienced with the young women he was sure to have impressed during his college football career.

There is, however, another, more important reason for Tom's desire to purchase status, a reason with roots deep in his birthplace in the Midwest, a region to which our attention is brought again and again. The importance of sign-exchange value for Tom, it can be argued, is largely a product of his desire to belong to a world that recognizes one necessary, if not sufficient, requirement for social prestige: one must be born and raised in the East. Without this "pedigree," Tom Buchanan's enormous wealth is just so much coin. Tom's fortune is not, as Roger Lewis would have it, "old money" (51). Although he inherited his wealth from an established Chicago family—so his money is not "new" in the sense of having been earned during his lifetime—an established Chicago family in the 1920s, the period in which the novel is set, would not have been considered "old" in the East, where America's "aristocracy" had lived since their forebears' initial immigration from Great Britain and Europe. For Easterners, in the 1920s at least, one of the requirements of old money was that it be earned not only in the past but in the East. To be from the Midwest was to be a *nouveau arrivé* in the eyes of Easterners, regardless of the size or age of one's fortune.

Having attended Yale, Tom must be, as Fitzgerald was, painfully aware of the Eastern social requirements he can never by birth fulfill; and even if he and Daisy return to Europe or the Midwest, Tom carries this knowledge inside himself, where it will always inform everything he does. He therefore seeks a status other than the one he can't have, a status that would declare his indifference to the issue of old money versus new. Thus his vulgarity—his lack of discretion with Myrtle Wilson; his loud, aggressive behavior; his rudeness—can be seen as an attempt to reassure himself that his money and power are all that count, an attempt to show that his wealth insulates him from considerations of class or refinement. The pseudoscientific "intellectualism" Tom adopts in referring Nick to a book he'd read about white civilization—as well as the racism endorsed by his reading—might be seen in this same light. He doesn't need to belong to old money because he belongs to a larger and more important group—the Aryan race: "We've produced all the things that go to make civilization—oh, science and art, and all that" (14; ch. 1).

A corollary of Tom's commodification of people is his ability to manipulate them very cold-bloodedly to get what he wants. In order to get Myrtle Wilson's sexual favors, he lets her think that he may marry her someday, that his hesitation is due to Daisy's alleged Catholicism rather than his own lack of desire. And in order to eliminate his rival for Daisy's affection, he sacrifices Gatsby to Wilson, whom he deliberately sends, armed and crazed, to Gatsby's house. (Tom's excuse to Nick—that he had no choice in the matter as Wilson was armed and Daisy was upstairs—wouldn't have prevented him from telephoning Gatsby to warn him.) In addition, Tom's sinister capabilities are hinted at through his familiarity with the underworld in the person of Walter Chase, who was involved in illegal activities with Gatsby. In fact, the last time we see Tom, we are led to associate him with Meyer Wolfsheim, the novel's most overtly sinister character. When Nick runs into Tom at the novel's close, he speculates that Tom's purpose in entering the jewelry store before which he is standing is "to buy a pearl necklace or perhaps only a pair of cuff buttons" (181; ch. 9). The pearl necklace, of course, reminds us of his commodification of women: either he's "paying an installment" on his purchase of Daisy, or he's "buying" another woman. The reference to cuff buttons, however, resonates powerfully with the human-molar cuff buttons of Meyer Wolfsheim.

It is no coincidence that Tom Buchanan has a very commodified psyche and very well-developed sinister capabilities. There is, in fact, a logical connection between these two aspects of personality, between commodity psychology and the cold-blooded manipulation of others. For exchange value demands subject-object (rather than subject-subject) relations among people: commodification is, by definition, the treatment of objects *and people* as commodities. From this perspective, Myrtle is merely a five-and-dime-store toy intended for the diversion of a rich white man who enjoys "slumming." Similarly, Daisy is merely Tom's property: it is quite right and natural for him to eliminate a trespasser—Gatsby—or, perhaps a more accurate articulation of Tom's viewpoint, to see that the debris that washed up on his shore is hauled away.

While a character such as Tom Buchanan is likely to make us sympathize with anyone who is dependent upon him, Daisy is not merely an innocent victim of her husband's commodified psyche. Rather, she and Tom are conspirators, from their marriage of convenience to their oft-noted tête-à-tête over cold chicken and ale in their pantry after Myrtle Wilson's death. In the first place, Daisy's acceptance of the pearls—and of the marriage to Tom they represent—is, of course, an act of commodification, a trade: she wanted Tom's sign-exchange value as much as he wanted hers. And, certainly, Daisy is capable, like Tom, of espousing an idea for the status she thinks it confers on her, as when she commodifies disaffection in order to impress Nick:

> "You see I think everything's terrible anyhow," she went on in a convinced way. "Everybody thinks so—the most advanced people. And I *know*. I've been everywhere and seen everything and done everything." Her eyes flashed around her in a defiant way, rather like Tom's. . . .
> The instant her voice broke off, ceasing to compel my attention, my belief, I felt the basic insincerity of what she had said. . . . I waited, and sure enough, in a moment she looked at me with an absolute smirk on her lovely face, as if she had asserted her membership in a rather distinguished secret society to which she and Tom belonged. (18; ch. 1)

Even Daisy's extramarital affair with Gatsby, like her earlier romance with him, has as its prerequisite her assumption that he is a member of her class, and when that assumption is challenged by Tom during the confrontation scene in the hotel suite, her enthusiasm for Gatsby dampens considerably. In short, Daisy can commodify with the best. Nevertheless, her primary use to us, in terms of commodity psychology, is not as a commodifier but as a commodity. An examination of Daisy's role as commodity—in addition to granting her a more complicated personality than she is often allowed[3]—foregrounds what the novel reveals about the social and psychological functions of woman as the object of male desire in a commodity culture.

According to Luce Irigaray, in a patriarchal society, women, like goods and signs, are commodities traded among men. Women "have value only in that they serve the possibility of, and potential benefit in, relations among men" (172). From this perspective, the social roles imposed on women, Irigaray believes, are limited to mother, virgin, and prostitute. Daisy, I think it can reasonably be argued, fills all three roles, sometimes separately, sometimes simultaneously, for different characters at different moments. Mothers, Irigaray explains, are

> reproductive instruments marked with the name of the father and enclosed in his house. . . . [They] must be private property, excluded from exchange. . . . [They] cannot circulate in the form of commodities without threatening the very existence of the social order. . . . Their responsibility is to maintain the social order without intervening so as to change it. (185)

This conception of the function of the mother in a patriarchy helps explain one of the roles in which Tom sees Daisy. Although his behavior toward his wife does not foreground her biological function as a reproductive instrument, Daisy nevertheless provides this function: she has a child who bears his name and she is capable of having others. More important in terms of the social implications of Irigaray's notion of the mother, Tom considers Daisy his private property, and his belief in the dependence of the social order on the inviolability of that role becomes ludicrously clear when he fears he may lose her to Gatsby: "I suppose the latest thing is to sit back and let Mr. Nobody from nowhere make love to your wife. Well, if that's the idea you can count me out. . . . Nowadays people begin by sneering at family life and family institutions and next they'll throw everything overboard and have intermarriage between black and white" (130; ch. 7). The importance to Tom personally of Daisy as his private property—as the Irigarayan mother—is evident in the great lengths to which he goes to keep her in that role, from his investigation into Gatsby's past, to his vicious verbal attack on his rival before Daisy, Nick, and Jordan in a hotel suite in New York, to his central role in Gatsby's murder.

Daisy also has many of the role functions of Irigaray's virgin. Although by the time we meet Daisy she is no longer a biological virgin, for both Tom and Gatsby she functions symbolically in that role. "*The virginal woman,*" writes Irigaray, "*is pure exchange value. . . .* In and of herself, she does not exist: she is a simple envelope veiling what is really at stake in social exchange" (186). I think it is safe to suggest that Irigaray's use of the term *exchange value* implicitly merges exchange value with sign-exchange value. For, as is especially clear in the case of Tom Buchanan and Jay Gatsby, relations among men, to which Irigaray refers woman's value, are semiotically saturated. Looked at from this point of view, it is not surprising that Tom often treats Daisy (until he fears losing her) as if she didn't exist. In her role as virgin, she has meaning for Tom only as sign, not as physical being. Daisy is the sign of the "good girl": she bears the name of a flower; she is always dressed in white; she always looks cool, even in hot weather. She has the appearance of the virginal, innocent woman a man marries for reasons related to social status. Tom also uses Daisy's sign-exchange value as virgin to define and inflate his relations with the numerous "bad girls" with whom he has affairs. His marriage to the sign of the virgin necessarily and conveniently circumscribes his adulterous relationships (he can't marry a bad girl because he's already married, and as he lies to Myrtle, his good girl doesn't believe in divorce) and defines them (deliciously) as cheating.

In addition, Daisy has a virginal role function in Gatsby's eyes. She is the symbol of the identity he wants to acquire and of the imaginary past he wants to substitute for his actual past; that is, she is the symbol of his virginal dream, the dream he keeps pure and untouched by time or circumstance. In his vision of Daisy, she, too, is untouched by the passage of time. From his perspective, she is never really touched by Tom: "She never loved you," he tells Tom; "in her heart she never loved any one except me" (131; ch. 7). Therefore, Gatsby cannot quite bring himself to believe that Daisy has a child: "He kept looking at the child with surprise," Nick informs us. "I don't think he had ever really believed in its existence before" (117; ch. 7).

Perhaps Daisy's most interesting function, at least in terms of commodity psychology, is her role as prostitute. "Prostitution," Irigaray explains, "amounts to usage that is exchanged. Usage that is not merely potential: it has already been realized" (186). "Usage that is exchanged" is, of course, one way to describe Daisy's marriage. In a very real sense, Daisy simply sold herself to the highest bidder. In addition, her use value, as sexual object, was "not merely potential" but had "already been realized" by the time she married Tom: although her husband didn't know it, she and Gatsby had already had sexual relations. Furthermore, Irigaray observes that "the woman's body is valuable *because* it has already been used. In the extreme case, the more it has served, the more it is worth" (186, my emphasis). This aspect of the prostitute role is part of what Gatsby finds particularly appealing about Daisy: "It excited him, too, that many men had already loved Daisy—it increased her value in his eyes" (148; ch. 8). It doesn't matter whether or not Daisy actually slept with any of these former lovers; the operative element here is that their love relations with her, whatever those relations were, increased her sign-exchange value for Gatsby. Her image as a woman "possessed" by other men, symbolically if not literally, increased his desire to possess her himself. Ironically, because Gatsby views all roles in terms of their sign-exchange value, Daisy's value as prostitute (as usage exchanged) enhances, in his eyes, her value as virgin (as pure sign-exchange value).

Daisy herself seems to understand all too well the significance of woman as commodity when she describes the birth of her daughter, Pammy, to Nick: "I woke up out of the ether with an utterly abandoned feeling, and asked the nurse right away if it was a boy or a girl. She told me it was a girl, and so I turned my head away and wept. 'All right,' I said, 'I'm glad it's a girl. And I hope she'll be a fool—that's the best thing a girl can be in this world, a beautiful little fool'" (17; ch. 1). This passage does not reveal, as Susan Resneck Parr believes, Daisy's "ennui"; nor is its significance circumscribed by Daisy's "recognition of just how painful intelligence and consciousness can be" (68). Rather, Daisy knows that a "beautiful little fool" is the best thing a girl can be because, given that woman is a commodity, she had better be marketable. Being beautiful and a fool is a very marketable combination. Also, if she is a fool, perhaps she won't know the despair of struggling against her fate, for perhaps she won't even suffer the awareness of her fate (one can be a commodity unconsciously as well as consciously). Thus it is a very particular kind of consciousness—consciousness of being female in a patriarchy—that Daisy recognizes as painful.

Daisy's speech in this excerpt is certainly a bitter lament for the condition of women in a man's world, but it is also an acceptance of that condition and a desire to see her daughter profit by it. Daisy's acceptance of women's oppression—that is, her belief that it is an inescapable given in what we today call a phallocentric culture—explains, in part, her willingness to commodify herself. In a gender war game in which the enemy has all the big guns, mere survival, which is all the Myrtle Wilsons of the world can hope for, is not enough for Daisy. She wants the same narcissistic reinforcements Tom wants—financial and social hegemony and the attention and esteem such success commands—and as a woman of her time and place, her quickest and surest method to achieve these desiderata is to commodify herself.

Just as Tom's commodity psychology is manifested in the ways in which he commodifies his world, Daisy's is manifested, in large part, in the ways in which she commodifies herself. In Daisy's case, however, the behavior that is most psychologically revealing is the behavior that is emotionally self-destructive, for even when her behavior is destructive of others, it is ultimately grounded in her own self-destructiveness.[4] Daisy's brand of self-destructive behavior is one familiar to many women and men, although in our culture it has been stereotypically associated with women: self-destructive love. Obviously, Daisy didn't love Tom when she married him or she wouldn't have tried to call off the marriage after receiving an overseas letter from Gatsby. By the time the couple returned from their three-month honeymoon, however, Jordan reports that she had "never seen a girl so mad about her husband" (78; ch. 4). The juxtaposition, in Jordan's narrative, of Daisy's prenuptial indifference with her posthoneymoon ardor forces the reader to wonder what happened in that short time to change Daisy's attitude so drastically. Is Daisy's alteration the result of marital bliss? Jordan's description of Tom's infidelity on their return from the honeymoon suggests a different answer. "'A week after I left Santa Barbara Tom ran into a wagon on the Ventura road one night, and ripped a front wheel off his car. The girl who was with him got into the papers, too, because her arm was broken—she was one of the chambermaids in the Santa Barbara Hotel'" (78; ch. 4).

Given this incident, and what we already know about Tom's affair with Myrtle, it is quite probable that by the time he and Daisy arrived in Santa Barbara, Daisy already knew that her husband was unfaithful. This would explain her discomfort whenever Tom was out of her sight: "If he left the room for a minute she'd look around uneasily, and say: 'Where's Tom gone?' and wear the most abstracted expression until she saw him coming in the door" (78; ch. 4). Surely, she had good reason to fear that unless he was with her, Tom might be pursuing another woman because he had already done so on their honeymoon. Rather than hate him for his mistreatment of her, however, Daisy falls in love with him: "She used to sit on the sand with his head in her lap by the hour, rubbing her fingers over his eyes and looking at him with unfathomable delight" (78; ch. 4). Daisy loves, as Sylvia Plath puts it, "the boot in the face" (223). Daisy loves the brute. And loving the brute is related to being a commodity.

By definition, a commodity is the object of the verb, not the subject: the commodity doesn't make a purchase; it is the purchase. That is, a commodity is never an agent. Furthermore, its sign-exchange value is a function not of anything inherent in itself but of the market's current rate of exchange. In terms of women as commodities in a male-dominated market, this means that the woman has no control over the definition of her own sign-exchange value. In the first place, she is not an agent; in the second place, her sign-exchange value doesn't reside in anything inherent in herself but is produced by the current rate of exchange among men. This state of affairs encourages low self-esteem in women, and the corollary of low self-esteem is self-destructiveness, especially in love: if I'm no good, then anyone who loves me must be of little or no value; the lover who is kind to me will ultimately be found lacking, but the lover who mistreats me thereby proves his worth. Enter Tom.

Although Gatsby is certainly more charming than Tom and Daisy, and more sympathetically portrayed by Nick, he nevertheless represents their desires in abstraction. However much the Buchanans' possessions are important to them in terms of sign-exchange value, they also have use value: we see the couple reclining on their sofas and eating at their tables. In contrast, we are told that the only room Gatsby occupies in his magnificently furnished mansion is his bedroom, which is "the simplest room of all" (3; ch. 1). We see him in this room only once, and even then his purpose is to show it to Daisy. He almost never uses his library, pool, or hydroplane himself; and he doesn't drink the alcohol or know most of the guests at his lavish parties. It seems that for the protagonist the sole function of material possessions is sign-exchange value: he wants the image their ownership confers on him and nothing more. For Gatsby, the commodity is commodity sign. Furthermore, while all three characters accumulate commodity signs, Gatsby's signs are almost all empty: his Gothic library filled with uncut books, his imitation Hôtel de Ville with its "spanking new" tower "under a thin beard of raw ivy" (5; ch. 1), his photo of himself at Oxford, are all surfaces without interiors. Finally, Gatsby's accumulation of empty signs—itself an abstraction—is performed in the service of another abstraction: the acquisition of

Daisy as a means of canceling his identity, annihilating his past, in order to become "his Platonic conception of himself" (99; ch. 6), that is, in order to become an abstraction himself.

Although Gatsby believes that his ultimate goal is the possession of Daisy—a belief Nick, Jordan, Tom, and Daisy seem to share—Daisy is merely the key to his goal rather than the goal itself. It is not "the absolute good" that Daisy embodies for the protagonist (Gallo 38), or even "beauty and innocence" (Chase 300), but the sign of her social class. What Gatsby really wants is to acquire the sign that he belongs to the same bright, spotless, airy, carefree world of the very rich that Daisy embodied for him when they first met. For Gatsby, her presence gave the house in which she lived a feeling of "breathless intensity,"

> a hint of bedrooms upstairs more beautiful and cool than other bedrooms, of gay and radiant activities taking place through its corridors, and of romances that were not musty and laid away already in lavender, but fresh and breathing and redolent of this year's shining motor-cars and of dances whose flowers were scarcely withered. (148; ch. 8).

That the rhetoric of this passage reveals the stereotypical, romance-magazine quality of Gatsby's desire for Daisy (Way 95) doesn't undercut the force of his desire. On the contrary, romance-magazine life—that is, life as a fiction in which the commodity sign is the avatar of happiness—is clearly what Gatsby seeks. Thus, in accumulating material goods in order to win Daisy, he is accumulating one kind of sign in order to acquire another.

What is there in Gatsby's background that makes Daisy such a powerful sign for him? The answer to this question can be found in Gatsby's boyhood with his parents and with Dan Cody. "James—that was really, or at least legally, his name. . . . His parents were shiftless and unsuccessful farm people—his imagination had never really accepted them as his parents at all. . . . So he invented just the sort of Jay Gatsby that a seventeen-year-old boy would be likely to invent" (98–99; ch. 6). What sort of a Jay Gatsby is that? In addition to the model we have of Gatsby as an adult—for he stayed faithful to his original conception "to the end" (99; ch. 6)—we have the clue his father gives us when he shows Nick "Jimmy's" boyhood "schedule," in which the young man divided his day, in the self-improvement tradition of Benjamin Franklin, among physical exercise, the study of electricity, work, sports, the practice of elocution and poise, and the study of needed inventions. This schedule suggests that he hoped—indeed planned—to live the "rags-to-riches" life associated with self-made millionaires like John D. Rockefeller and Andrew Carnegie. And he received his first exposure to wealth, and his first opportunity to better himself, when he went to work for Dan Cody, a rags-to-riches man himself. But Gatsby's conception of a life of wealth and leisure was, at this time, rather flat, uninspired, a product of the conceptual domain rather than of direct personal experience. For until he met Daisy, there had always been "indiscernible barbed wire" (148; ch. 8) between him and the wealthy people he'd met through Dan Cody.

Thus, Gatsby had set his sights on the attainment of wealth and social status long before he knew Daisy, but these achievements revealed their ultimate psychological payoff only upon meeting her. His contact with her let him imagine what it would *feel* like to be a member of her world, to be, as he felt Daisy was, "gleaming like silver, safe and proud above the hot struggles of the poor" (150; ch. 8), the struggle that he, himself, had endured and hated. This feeling—the feeling of being insulated from his own past and from the existential inwardness his awareness of that past engenders—is what she came to represent for him, and this is what he wants in wanting Daisy. He therefore insists that Daisy admit she never loved Tom and that they be married from her parents' home in Louisville—so that they can, as Gatsby says, "repeat the past" and "fix everything just the way it was before" and so that Gatsby can, as Nick observes, "recover something, some idea of himself perhaps, that had gone into loving Daisy" (111; ch. 6).

The "idea of himself" he wants to recover is that of the young man who believed his own fantasy about his upper-class origins, who belonged to Daisy's world because she believed that he belonged, "that he was a person from much the same stratum as herself" (149; ch. 8). Possessing Daisy again five years later would, in Gatsby's eyes, "launder" his "new money" and make it "old," would make his "spanking new" imitation Hôtel de Ville an ancestral seat. In this way, Gatsby's possession of Daisy would undo history and cancel his identity, allowing him to deny there had ever been a time when he didn't have money and position—to believe his lie to Nick that he was from a wealthy family and had gone to Oxford and toured Europe—and to believe that he had never lost this world because he had never lost Daisy to Tom. If he could cancel his identity, replace his historical past with a fictional past, then he could eliminate the existential pain that accompanies an awareness of lack, loss, or limitation. He could be insulated, as he believes

Daisy is insulated, in that magical world of fresh romances and shining motorcars and flowers that never wither, that fictional world Gatsby created five years ago and "store[d] up in his ghostly heart" (97; ch. 5).

Like Tom, Gatsby aggressively pursues what he desires, and the cold-blooded nature of his pursuit is, also like Tom's, a function of commodity psychology. The signs of luxury, carefree pleasure, and sensual beauty among which Gatsby circulates do not exist in a vacuum. They are supported by a very dark and sinister world of corruption, crime, and death. Certainly Gatsby's wealth, as Nick and Tom learn, is derived from underworld activities, specifically bootlegging and fraudulent bonds. This is not "the no-man's land between business and criminality" Gatsby may think it is (Way 89); it is the underworld of Meyer Wolfsheim, who has such unlimited criminal connections that he was able to "fix" the 1919 World Series. And this is the man who takes credit for giving Gatsby his start.

We get a glimpse of this world in the "villainous"-looking servants Wolfsheim sends to work for Gatsby and in the phone calls Gatsby receives (and which, after Gatsby's death, Nick receives by accident) from obvious criminal sources. This is a world of predators and prey in which illegal—and thus often imperfect—liquor is sold over the counter to anyone with the money to pay for it, and in which fake bonds are passed in small towns to unsuspecting investors. Some of the people who buy the liquor may become ill from it; some may die. All of the small investors who buy the fraudulent bonds will lose money that they probably can't afford to lose. And when the inevitable mistakes are made and the law steps in, someone will have to be sacrificed, as Gatsby sacrifices Walter Chase.

Even the protagonist's desire for Daisy—which many readers use to support their romantic view of him—is informed by an underworld weltanschauung: when Gatsby first courted Daisy at her parents' home in Louisville, "he took what he could get, ravenously and unscrupulously—eventually he took Daisy" (149; ch. 8). Gatsby did not make love to Daisy; he "took" her "ravenously and unscrupulously." This language resonates strongly with his dubious association with Dan Cody before meeting Daisy and with his criminal activities subsequent to their initial affair.

Gatsby, like Tom, treats people as commodities. The people who buy his liquor and fraudulent bonds, or who, like Walter Chase, get caught doing his dirty work, are merely pawns, stepping-stones, objects to be exchanged for what he wants: in Gatsby's case, the money to support his quest to acquire the sign that will cancel history and thereby relieve him of the existential burden of his own existence. However, although Gatsby is the subject in his subject-object dealings with his criminal connections and in his commodification of Daisy, he is also an object in his relationship with her, a point that Judith Fetterly misses in her interesting analysis of Daisy and Jordan as the novel's scapegoats. Gatsby commodifies himself—he adopts an image and a life-style in order to "sell" himself—in order to be accepted as a member of Daisy's social stratum. Furthermore, his desire for Daisy mirrors her desire for Tom. As we have seen, Daisy's obsession with Tom began only after she became aware of his involvement with other women, and Gatsby's desire for Daisy was enhanced by his knowledge that she had been loved by other men. Significantly, it wasn't until he had had sexual relations with her and she remained unmoved—"betray[ing]" him by "vanish[ing] into her rich house, into her rich, full life"—that Gatsby began to pursue Daisy as if he had "committed himself to the following of a grail" (149; ch. 8).

While subject-object relations are necessarily a dominant value in a culture in which money—and the power over others it produces—is the *sine qua non* of happiness, commodity psychology is even more closely related to the novel's emergent value: object-object relations, the most abstract form of human relations and the one that is dramatized in Gatsby's relationship with Daisy. If subject-subject relations can be said to exist at all in the novel, they exist as a residual value, a function of nostalgia and fantasy, as when Gatsby reminisces about his initial encounters with Daisy or imagines their future together.

If subject-object relations produce the distance from others that facilitates cold-blooded manipulation and exploitation, object-object relations produce distance from oneself. As we have seen, in constituting oneself as an object for the other, one knows oneself primarily through the eyes of the other, that is, primarily as a surface rather than an interior. One is thus liberated from the burden of existential self-reflection. It is not surprising, in this context, that Fitzgerald was unable to provide us with the inner history of Gatsby and Daisy's Long Island affair. As the author himself notes, in a letter to Edmund Wilson, he "had no feeling about or knowledge of . . . the emotional relations between Gatsby and Daisy from the time of their reunion to the catastrophe" (*Letters* 341–42). Clearly, Fitzgerald could not represent the inwardness of the couple's relationship because there is none. There is only the interaction of two surfaces. Appropriately, the only interchanges described between the pair occur in relation to, and are mediated by, Gatsby's commodity signs: his reunion with Daisy in Nick's cottage, in a setting painstakingly prepared for that purpose; Daisy's grand tour of his mansion; and the couple's mutual display over his collection of expensive shirts. It is as a surface without an interior that James Gatz's creation lives his dream of happiness with Daisy, and it is as a surface without an interior that "'Jay Gatsby' [breaks] up like glass against Tom's hard malice" (148; ch. 8).

One of the central paradoxes of the American dream, then, is that while it claims to open history to everyone, to allow each individual the opportunity to become a part of American history, in reality it closes off history: it allows each individual the opportunity to escape from history into the commodity. Thus, for Gatsby, the commodity—not just his material possessions but Daisy as well—becomes the site of displacement, the sign he needs to acquire if he is to feel in control, protected, insulated from the existential inwardness that accompanies his psychological connection to his own past. That is, the commodity becomes, as Lily Bart's aestheticized body is for her and Lawrence Selden, a religious relic, the site of mystification, of magical thinking. It is interesting to note in this context that readers who romanticize Gatsby, as Gatsby himself does, share the character's desire to sever himself from his own history. Richard Chase, for example, sees Gatsby as part of "an earlier pastoral ideal," in that he shares, with Natty Bumppo, Huck Finn, and Ishmael, an "ideal of innocence, escape, and the purely personal code of conduct" (301).[5] Gatsby may indeed "stand for America itself" (L. Trilling 240) as the "projected wish fulfillment" of the "consciousness of a race" (Troy 21), but it is an America that is willing to exploit the underdog to advance its own interests and a consciousness that relates to others as commodities. Clearly, the desire to sever Gatsby from his exploitative history is accompanied by the desire to sever America from its.

Operating against *The Great Gatsby*'s powerful critique of commodity psychology is the novel's subtle reinforcement of the commodity's seductive appeal. This countermovement operates on two levels. First, because Nick is seduced by the dream Gatsby represents for him, his narrative seduces many readers into collusion with Gatsby's desire. Second, the language used to describe the physical setting of this world of wealth makes it attractive despite people like the Buchanans who populate it. Nick may like to think he disapproves of Jay Gatsby—because he knows he *should* disapprove of him for the same reasons he disapproves of the Buchanans—but it is clear from the beginning that the narrator is charmed by him. As Nick tells us, "There was something gorgeous about him, some heightened sensitivity to the promises of life. . . . it was an extraordinary gift for hope, a romantic readiness such as I have never found in any other person and which it is not likely I shall ever find again" (2; ch. 1).

This romantic vision of Gatsby is foregrounded in Nick's narrative through his focus on Gatsby's romantic images: the rebellious boy, the ambitious young roughneck, the idealistic dreamer, the devoted lover, the brave soldier, the lavish host. Gatsby's criminal connections are acknowledged, but because of Nick's response to them, they don't influence his opinion of the man. For example, Nick's manner of discussing Gatsby's criminal life tends to deflect attention away from the moral implications of Gatsby's underworld activities, as when Nick reports the following conversation he overheard at one of Gatsby's parties: "'He's a bootlegger,' said the young ladies, moving somewhere between his cocktails and his flowers" (61; ch. 4). The rhetoric of this phrase is typical of Nick's defense of Gatsby against his detractors, even when those detractors are right: his statement focuses on Gatsby's generosity and on the willingness to abuse it of those who gossip about him, thereby sidestepping the fact that "his cocktails and his flowers" weren't rightfully his at all: they were purchased with funds obtained from the sale of bootlegged liquor and fraudulent bonds.

Similarly, Nick influences reader reaction to Gatsby by his own emotional investment in those events that show Gatsby in a good light. For example, when Gatsby, confronted by Tom, admits in front of everyone that his Oxford experience was provided by a government arrangement for American soldiers who remained in Europe after World War I, Nick "wanted to get up and slap him on the back" (130; ch. 7). This small concession to reality on Gatsby's part elicits in Nick a renewal "of complete faith in him" (130; ch. 7). Despite what Nick knows about the underworld sources of Gatsby's wealth, despite the "unaffected scorn" Nick says he has for Gatsby's world, Gatsby himself is "exempt" from Nick's disapprobation: "Gatsby turned out all right at the end; it is what preyed on Gatsby, what foul dust floated in the wake of his dreams" (2;

ch. 1) that elicits Nick's disaffection—and that of many readers. It is easy to be influenced by the warmth of Nick's feelings because these feelings so strongly inform the portrait he paints. Like Nick, many of us would like to bask in Gatsby's smile, "one of those rare smiles with a quality of eternal reassurance in it . . . with an irresistible prejudice in your favor" (48; ch. 3).

Why should Nick deceive himself, and us, about Gatsby? Why should he foreground all the positive, likable qualities in Gatsby's personality and shift responsibility for the unpleasant ones onto others' shoulders? Certainly, it is not simply, as A. E. Dyson claims, Nick's "humanity" that "forces him to understand and pity Gatsby" (115). Rather, I think it is because the narrator is, himself, seduced by Gatsby's dream. At the age of thirty, and still being financed by his father while he tries to figure out what he should do with himself, it is not surprising that Nick wants to believe life still holds promise because he is afraid that it doesn't. He fears that all he has to look forward to is, as he puts it, "a thinning list of single men to know, a thinning briefcase of enthusiasm, thinning hair" (136; ch. 7). With one failed romance back home and one in New York, Nick wants to believe that the possibility of romance still exists. With his summer in New York—his latest in a series of adventures—having ended in disaster, he wants to believe in the possibility of hope. Nick believes in Gatsby because he wants to believe that Gatsby's dream can come true for himself: that a young man at loose ends can make the kind of outrageous financial success of himself that Gatsby has made . . . and seem to fall so completely in love with a woman . . . and be so optimistic about the future.

Clearly, in terms of the psychology of the narrator's desire, Dyson is very mistaken in his assertion that Carraway's "emotions and destiny are not centrally involved" in his narration (115). Nick's emotions and destiny are indeed centrally involved: he doesn't want to be reminded that Gatsby's glittering world rests on corruption because he wants that world for himself. He is in collusion with Gatsby's desire and leads readers into collusion with that desire as well. Following Nick's lead, for example, Tom Burnam says that Gatsby "survives sound and whole in character, uncorrupted by the corruption which surrounded him" (105). In a similar fashion, Rose Adrienne Gallo believes that Gatsby "maintained his innocence" to the end (43). Perhaps, like Nick, such readers want to believe that the protagonist's dream is inviolate because they want to believe that a dream like his can still come true. Nick's portrait of Gatsby is thus one reason why he is considered, as we have seen, such an appealing figure.

It is interesting to note that the question of Nick's reliability problematizes the question of narrator reliability in general: even if Nick were reliable (in that his views concerning the characters and events of the story represented Fitzgerald's views), we would still be left with the question of whether or not Fitzgerald understood all the implications of his own text. That is, the question of a narrator's reliability sidesteps the issue of how the author's unconscious is involved in producing the text. Even if Fitzgerald intended Nick as a reliable narrator who accurately portrays the Gatsby the author wanted us to see—even if Fitzgerald wanted us to believe, with Nick, that "Gatsby turned out all right at the end" and to save our disapprobation, as Nick does, for "what preyed on Gatsby, what foul dust floated in the wake of his dreams" (2; ch. 1)— we would still bear the burden of evaluating Gatsby's behavior beyond the limits of Nick's viewpoint because Fitzgerald's representation of both narrator and protagonist may have exceeded his intention. As we saw earlier, in Fitzgerald's letter to Edmund Wilson—and as we'll see later, in Arthur Miller's comments on *Death of a Salesman*—authorial intention, which is the locus and limit of the reliable narrator's function, is but a part of artistic creation. A good deal more of the text is produced by what the author doesn't (consciously) know. Thus, one might speculate that Fitzgerald's conflicted attitude toward the wealthy, or Miller's conflicted attitude toward his father, could have produced characterizations much less positive than either author (consciously) intended.

The reader appeal of Gatsby's desire to belong to the magic world in which Daisy is so at home—"Gatsby has possessed what the reader must also desire: the orgiastic present" (Dillon 61)—is also a testimonial to the power of the commodity. Gatsby may not make the best use of his mansion, his hydroplane, his swimming pool, and his library, but many of us might feel that *we* certainly would. In a novel in which the only alternative to the life-style of the wealthy is the valley of ashes (Nick's Midwest hardly qualifies as an alternative because the description of it is brief, sketchy, and focused on his nostalgia for a symbolic return to an innocent past that may no longer be possible for him), the commodity is rendered especially attractive by contrast. Furthermore, the commodity's appeal is powerfully reinforced for the reader by the language used to describe this world of leisure and luxury. Consumer goods are invested with magic—with the capacity to transform reality—which suggests that the material world is *itself* transcendent. Even the refreshments at Gatsby's parties, for example, seem enchanted: a "tray of cocktails floated at us through the twilight" (43; ch. 3), and on "buffet tables garnished with glistening hors-d'oeuvre, spiced baked hams crowded against salads of harlequin designs and pastry pigs and turkeys bewitched to a dark gold" (39–40; ch. 3). As John S. Whitley notes, in comparing the work of Fitzgerald and Keats, the description of Gatsby's buffet table

> creates an effect greater than that of mere opulence. The transmutation of base reality has already begun; nothing is quite what it seems. The pigs are made of pastry, the turkeys are a colour rather from the world of aesthetics than the world of cuisine and the salads are of "harlequin" designs, a word suggesting not merely a variety of colours but also masks and jokes. (24)

The commodity is especially compelling in the following description of the Buchanans' home on East Egg:

> Their house was . . . a cheerful red-and-white Georgian Colonial mansion, overlooking the bay. . . . The front was broken by a line of French windows, glowing now with reflected gold and wide open to the warm windy afternoon. . . . the front vista . . . [included] in its sweep a sunken Italian garden, a half acre of deep, pungent roses, and a snub-nosed motor-boat that bumped the tide offshore. . . .
> We walked through a high hallway into a bright rosy-colored space, fragilely bound into the house by French windows at either end. . . . A breeze blew through the room, blew curtains in at one end and out the other like pale flags, twisting them up toward the frosted wedding-cake of the ceiling, and then rippled over the wine-colored rug, making a shadow on it as wind does on the sea. (6–8; ch. 1)

This passage is a delicious appeal to every one of the five senses. The language is so sensual that the house seems to breathe with a life of its own, capable even of conquering nature, which it subdues and uses to enhance itself: "The lawn started at the beach and ran toward the front door for a quarter of a mile, jumping over sun-dials and brick walks and burning gardens—finally when it reached the house drifting up the side in bright vines as though from the momentum of its run" (6–7; ch. 1).

Although the estate is on the edge of the sea, one of the most powerful natural forces on earth, nature, in this passage, is utterly domesticated. The wild grasses that normally border the ocean have been replaced by a lawn, which jumps over objects like a trained dog, while vines decorate the house like jewelry. The commodity is so powerful that it can disenfranchise nature: nature becomes a commodity; the natural object becomes a human artifact valued for the money and prestige it represents. This setting thus has an existence independent of the characters who inhabit it: the estate doesn't need Tom and Daisy in order to be gorgeous; it was gorgeous before Tom bought it and it will be gorgeous after the Buchanans are gone. In fact, we could easily, and happily, imagine this place without its occupants. That is, the setting is bigger than the Buchanans—it contains and exceeds them. They neither use it up nor exhaust its possibilities. And it is impervious to their corruption: we are not led to associate the place with the events that occur there. Therefore, it exerts a magnetic appeal on many readers.[6]

This double movement—the text's simultaneous criticism of and fascination with the commodity—is largely responsible for the problematic nature of the novel's oft-quoted closing passage:

> . . . I became aware of the old island here that flowered once for Dutch
> sailors' eyes—a fresh, green breast of the new world. Its vanished trees,
> the trees that had made way for Gatsby's house, had once pandered in
> whispers to the last and greatest of all human dreams; for a transitory
> enchanted moment man must have held his breath in the presence of
> this continent, compelled into an aesthetic contemplation he neither
> understood nor desired, face to face for the last time in history with
> something commensurate to his capacity for wonder. (182; ch. 9)

Although Nick reminds us that the "fresh, green breast of the new world," that setting "commensurate to [our] capacity for wonder," "vanished" to make "way for Gatsby's home"—that is, was obliterated by the commodity—he also associates this "enchanted" dream of the Dutch sailors with Gatsby's commodified dream: "And as I sat there brooding on the old, unknown world, I thought of Gatsby's wonder when he first picked out the green light at the end of Daisy's dock" (182; ch. 9). The romantic sublime of the sailors' vision is thus tied to the commodity, in the form of Gatsby, in a way that makes the two—affectively if not logically—almost impossible to untangle. And, of course, the word *pandered* is associated with selling, carrying with it the promise to satisfy corrupt ambitions. Even the Dutch sailors' dream contains the power of and desire for the commodity embedded in it. As we know from history, these men came to the new world in search of goods and markets for prosperous Dutch merchants. Their purpose was material, not spiritual. While the sailors were awestruck by what they found, theirs was not an experience of romantic union with a sympathetic Nature such as their descendants would know in the nineteenth century. Rather, the sailors were *"compelled* into an aesthetic contemplation [they] *neither understood nor desired"* (182; ch. 9, my emphasis). This is the language, not of a postindustrial nostalgia for country life, but of a response to the wilderness as totally Other. Their success in subduing the vast otherness that was this continent bespeaks the power of the commodity to transform all otherness into the familiar, the domesticated, the safe. There is nothing so great or so wonderful that it can't be subdued by, and put into the service of, the commodity.

What happens once the commodity has domesticated nature, as it has in *The Great Gatsby*? Must the commodity itself take the place of nature as some kind of Other, just as the green light at the end of the Buchanans' dock substitutes for the green breast of the new world? The answer, I think, is both yes and no. Certainly, there is in our culture the desire to have the commodity perform this function. For if the commodity becomes Other, then we can at once "have" otherness and domesticate it. That is, we can at once have the Other as the sign of that which is not us/ours—investing it with all the desire and longing that keep us looking toward an imagined future fulfillment—and we can disempower that Other so that it is not threatening. In both cases, the commodity as Other is a means of avoiding existential inwardness: the desire and longing that keep us looking toward an imagined future fulfillment help distract us from the existential contingency of the present; a disempowered, nonthreatening Other means that even the unknown can't frighten us. Desire is thus submitted to its history: just as the commodity domesticates nature, so it domesticates desire. That is, not only is otherness domesticated by the commodity, but so is our *desire* for otherness. As I will argue in chapter 5, Joseph Heller shows us that an existential understanding of desire cannot survive a history dominated by the commodity. However, Fitzgerald, as we have seen, both submits desire to its history and refuses to submit it—and he doesn't seem to see the contradiction. For as much as he is the critic of the commodity, Fitzgerald is also the poet of the commodity. And his poetry attracts many readers to the very thing that, on a more overt level, the novel condemns. Thus, while *The Great Gatsby* offers a significant critique of the American dream's commodified ideology, it also repackages and markets that dream anew. This double movement of the text gives the closing line a special irony: if we do "beat on, boats against the current, borne back ceaselessly into the past," there is in this novel that which strengthens the backflow, bearing us ceaselessly back into the commodity. For although Gatsby fails to realize the dream, many readers continue to invest in it.

3

The Commodity Comes Home to Roost

Repression, Regression, and Death in Arthur Miller's *Death of a Salesman*

Since *Death of a Salesman*'s New York premiere in 1949, critics have tended to view Arthur Miller's remarkable play in one of two ways: as a psychological drama or as a Marxist critique of capitalist culture. Despite the play's rather obvious psychoanalytic content—the drama is structured by a series of detailed descriptions of the stages in Willy Loman's psychological breakdown—most critics treat the work's psychological dimension in terms of its tragic, rather than psychoanalytic, function. The psychological drama, the argument goes, foregrounds the protagonist's responsibility for his failure as a husband and father and is thematically centered on the scene in which Willy commits adultery in a Boston hotel room. As Giles Mitchell puts it, Willy's failures are "preeminently personal" (394). Similarly, Leonard Moss argues that "Miller's technical apparatus—the colloquial language, the symbolic images, and the dramatized recollections—shapes the pride and blindness of a mentality, not the evil influence of a social condition" (36).[1] The play's Marxist critique of capitalist culture, on the other hand, is said to foreground the protagonist's victimization by an uncaring society obsessed with material success and to center thematically on the scene in which Willy is cold-bloodedly fired by Howard Wagner.[2] Those critics who have addressed the coexistence of both dimensions in the play have generally done so in order to show how the two are at odds, observing that the psychological drama and the political critique rest on mutually exclusive assumptions and that each reading depends for its strength on the weakness of the other.[3]

This polarization of the play's psychological and political dimensions misunderstands, I believe, the nature of the overarching mythos that, as everyone ironically acknowledges, informs Miller's play: the mythos of the American dream. As this chapter will attempt to show, it is in the American dream—specifically, in its relation to commodity psychology—that the play's psychological and political strands are inextricably entwined. For the American dream serves as the "ore" from which Willy fashions the ideological armor he uses to disguise and deny his psychological problems and those of his family in order to escape the existential inwardness that such a self-awareness would force upon him. This dialectical relationship between the individual psyche and the socius is manifest at those points where the play's psychological and ideological content intersect most clearly: Willy's commodification of personal image; his five so-called memory scenes, which, I will argue, are regressive episodes the structural similarities of which underscore their psychological importance; and the Loman family's sexuality, which is an important, though critically neglected, aspect of this work. In addition, I will suggest that the intersection of psychology and ideology can be observed, in more speculative terms, in the rather one-sided reading of Willy Loman that has dominated the critical literature and in the playwright's own apparent emotional investment in his protagonist, which is revealed in the interaction of the play's realist and expressionist episodes.

Certainly, the most obvious example of Willy's ideological armor, and the one that informs all the psychological events that structure the play, is his commodification of personal image. For him, the road to the American dream is paved with a winning personality: "That's the wonder, the wonder of this country," the protagonist tells his young sons, "that a man can end with diamonds here on the basis of being liked!" (79; act 2). Because, as Willy observes, a rich man is always well liked, being well liked, he concludes, must be how poor men become wealthy. For this reason, he believes that being well liked is the necessary and sufficient currency for purchasing success in the business world. Of course, Willy's logic depends on a very superficial view of what it means to be well liked. Because he substitutes form for content—"It's not what you say, it's how you say it" (58; act 1)—he mistakes the image of popularity for the reality, ignoring, for example, the obvious fact that, for some rich men, being "well liked" is not the source of their wealth but its effect. (As Charley next door says of the financial scoundrel J. P. Morgan, "with his pockets on he was very well liked" [90; act

2.]) But superficial is Willy's middle name: for him, success and the image of success are one. He "regularly confuses labels with reality," implying, for example, "that a punching bag is good because, as he says, 'It's got Gene Tunney's signature on it'" (Weales 133). It's the image of success Willy tries to project by joking with his customers and by exaggerating his sales prowess, and it's the image of success—the appearance of being well liked—that he teaches his sons is the necessary and sufficient commodity to ensure their future success in the business world, the world that Willy is certain will fulfill his dreams.

As Biff observes, however, Willy "had the wrong dreams" (132; Requiem). We must wonder, although the question is rarely raised, why the protagonist chose—and why, at all costs, he clings to—his dream of business success when his ability and his pleasure clearly lie in working with his hands. The answer can be found in the American dream's promise to remediate Willy's ontological insecurity, his lack of "any unquestionable self-validating certainties" (Laing 39), which has apparently plagued him since his abandonment in early childhood by his father and older brother Ben. The early loss of these two role models, with whose idealized memory Willy could never compete, has left him, in his own words, feeling "kind of temporary about [him]self" (46; act 1) or, in psychoanalytic terms, narcissistically wounded—humiliated by his own powerlessness.[4] The resulting need for a reassuring father explains the otherwise mystifying importance for Willy of the Dave Singleman story: the old salesman, whose popularity and resourcefulness allowed him to make a good living even at the age of eighty-four, fits Willy's idealized image of his own father. The protagonist's obsession with image throughout the play underscores this insecurity, for it bespeaks the narcissist, the man who must continually bolster the surface of his personality by finding its positive reflection in the world around him because that surface has no firm ground of its own to support it from within.

Narcissism also explains why Willy refuses to relinquish, no matter what the cost to himself or his family, the personal image of the successful salesman he has manufactured from the ideological fabric of the American dream. It is not merely shame he fears, but the loss of a coherent self, for an idealized self-image is the sine qua non of the narcissist's identity.[5] Such a shaky structure requires the kind of ego reinforcement Willy desires: the admiration of financially successful, powerful men like his brother, the admiration one receives for achieving the American dream's rags-to-riches metamorphosis. Thus, Willy's failure to see the obvious unscrupulous underside of Ben's financial success, like the rest of his apparent moral confusion concerning his and his sons' success-oriented ethics, is the result, not of an "ignorance of the world and . . . a naiveté so colossal as to amount to a kind of innocence" (Mitchell 406), but of selective perception. The protagonist's overwhelming psychological need for ontological reassurance doesn't permit him to see anything that might inhibit his pursuit of the business success that promises to supply that reassurance.

The only place Willy was ever able to market his personal image successfully was in his home. As we see in his memories of his boys' high-school days, Willy's young sons, Biff and Happy, adored their father. They believed all his stories about his popularity, his sales achievements, and the business of his own that he would have someday so that he'd be able to stay home with his family instead of spending his work-week on the road as he had done all his life. In their eyes, he was the success he pretended to be, and their belief in him helped him to deny the reality of his small sales commissions. If young Biff and Happy kept their father's image shining for him, Linda, Willy's wife, always kept it in good repair by helping her husband deny unpleasant realities. As we can see in the following memory scene, which closely resembles her behavior in the play's present-tense action as well, Linda refused to acknowledge any of Willy's weaknesses and wouldn't let him acknowledge them either:

> Willy: . . . My God, if business don't pick up I don't know what I'm gonna do!
> Linda: Well, next week you'll do better.
> Willy: Oh, I'll knock 'em dead next week. I'll go to Hartford. I'm very well liked in Hartford. You know, the trouble is, Linda, people don't seem to take to me. . . .
> Linda: Oh, don't be foolish.
> Willy: I know it when I walk in. They seem to laugh at me. . . . I talk too much. . . .
> Linda: You don't talk too much, you're just lively.
> Willy, *smiling*: Well, I figure, what the hell, life is short, a couple of jokes. . . . (30–31; act 1)

If Linda provides "the spiritual glue that holds together [Willy's] rickety frame" (Schlueter and Flanagan 59), it's nevertheless a service of dubious value she performs. By functioning, in effect, as a manic defense against the physical and psychological realities that continually threaten to invade her husband's awareness, Linda prevents him from challenging his own self-delusions and thereby helps preclude the possibility of his psychological growth.

That we must rely on Willy's memories for much of what we know of Linda is one of the reaons why she is such a problematic character. Certainly, when she speaks for herself in the present, she reveals that she is aware of her husband's faults and simply loves him in spite of them. Nevertheless, I think the tendency of some readers to idealize her—to believe, for example, that "she is just too good for Willy and thus too good for the play" (Welland 49)—ignores the role Linda's own desire may play in her collusion with Willy's project to escape existential inwardness. At best, of course, she wants to maintain Willy's self-delusion because she believes it would be more disastrous for him to face the truth about himself; at worst, however, her purpose is to keep the truth about the severity of her husband's psychological problems hidden from herself so that she, too, can avoid the existential inwardness such a realization might force upon her. In either case, by helping Willy deny the physical and psychological realities of his life, Linda exacerbates her husband's problems.

It is Willy's struggle with those realities, brought to the fore by the double trauma of mounting pressures at the office and Biff's visit home, that constitutes the five expressionistic episodes in which he seems to remember or imagine events from his past. However, these episodes are not a function simply of memory or imagination. They are, rather, psychological regressions, which, in pathological cases like Willy's, involve "a full hallucinatory cathexis of the perceptive system" (Freud *Interpretation of Dreams* 496). As D. W. Winnicott explains, regression involves not the imagining but the "*reliving* of dream and memory situations" (288, my emphasis) which opens the psyche to new possibilities. Although, in the therapeutic encounter, the regressed subject relives early childhood episodes, Winnicott's description of regression closely parallels, and illuminates, Willy Loman's behavior.

Like Winnicott's patients, Willy has developed a "false self" (Winnicott 281)—his successful-salesman persona—to defend against what Winnicott calls an "original environmental-failure situation" (287), in this case, Willy's childhood loss of father and older brother. The existence of this false self "results in [a] sense of futility" (292), which the protagonist recurrently manifests throughout the play. Furthermore, regression can involve a return either to a pleasant past experience, such as Willy's happy times with his young family, or to a painful episode from the past, such as his initial falling-out with Biff in the Boston hotel room. Most important for our understanding of the protagonist, "regression is distinct from the other defence organizations in that it carries with it . . . a new opportunity for an unfreezing of the [failure] situation and a chance for . . . spontaneous recovery" (Winnicott 283). Because regression involves a return to the experience that lies at the bottom of a current conflict, as it does in each of Willy's five regressive episodes, it allows the regressed person to become aware of the concrete source of a heretofore baffling psychological condition. Recovery, in this context, means the acquisition of a new attitude toward oneself and one's problems based on the insight gained during the regression. Thus, in offering the opportunity to live an authentic relationship to one's conflicts, regression always offers the opportunity to acquire or deepen existential inwardness. From this perspective, Willy's five regressive episodes represent five opportunities for him to alter his course, both psychologically and existentially, and it is significant that his response, in each case, is the same. For, as we shall see, the pattern formed by his responses to regression reveals a systematic, if only partly conscious, effort on Willy's part to eschew the existential inwardness increasingly pressed upon him by the accumulated refuse of his psyche.

The first three regressive episodes follow roughly the same pattern: each time Willy is confronted with a traumatic reality in the present, he regresses to a time when his American-dream fantasies could still convince him and his family that he was the success he wanted to be. Thus, as we see in his first regression, which occurs shortly after his return home from his aborted attempt to drive to New England (20–34; act 1), the protagonist tries to escape the present reality of having been taken off salary and put on straight commission by regressing to a time when his young sons, still in high school, polished his car and hung on his every word, a time when he could still look to the future with hope. In his second regression, which occurs during and after his card game with Charley later that night (38–46; act 1), Willy tries to escape his present pain over Biff's life as a drifter and his own inability to help his son by regressing to a time when he was able to show off his boys' high-spiritedness and filial devotion in front of his brother Ben: he imagines sending the boys off to steal sand from a nearby construction site in order to rebuild the front stoop. In his third regression, which occurs in Howard Wagner's office (77–83; act 1), the protagonist tries to escape the present trauma of being fired by regressing to a time when he had the opportunity to superintend Ben's Alaskan timberland: "God, timberland! Me and my boys in those grand outdoors!" (78; act 1).

None of these three visions of the past, however, provides the escape Willy seeks. For it is during such regressive experiences that repressed conflicts tend to erupt.[6] Thus, his first regressive vision of his happy young family is inevitably interrupted by the memory that Biff had been an irresponsible boy and a petty thief whose behavior was often wild and selfish:

> Bernard, *entering on the run*: Where is [Biff]? If he doesn't study!
> Willy, *moving to the forestage, with great agitation*: You'll give him the answers!
> Bernard: I do, but I can't on a Regents! That's a state exam! They're liable to arrest me!
> Willy: Where is he? I'll whip him, I'll whip him!
> Linda: And he'd better give back that football, Willy, it's not nice.
> Willy: Biff! Where is he? Why is he taking everything?
> Linda: He's too rough with the girls, Willy. All the mothers are afraid of him!
> Willy: I'll whip him. (33–34; act 1)

Similarly, Willy's second pleasant regression is interrupted by his fear that he didn't raise his sons right. He imagines telling Ben, "Sometimes I'm afraid that I'm not teaching them the right kind of—Ben, how should I teach them?" (46; act 1). Finally, Willy's third regressive episode is interrupted by the memory that he'd refused the opportunity to manage Ben's Alaskan timberland: Linda's repetition of his story about the successful Dave Singleman convinced him to keep his job.

In terms of Willy's psychological experience, readers' concern over whether or not the past events he recalls are accurately reported according to some standard of objective reality is irrelevant. What matters is that the conflicts' emergence reveals Willy's experience of them; it is subjective reality that is revelatory here. For these eruptions of repressed conflicts are a product of Willy's present psychological state as well as a reflection of his former condition. During a traumatic period, conflicts that have been long buried tend to surface and demand attention or discharge. This is, of course, why regression often functions as a tool of psychological growth: it brings forward into consciousness, and allows the subject the opportunity to work on, conflicts that have heretofore inhabited the unconscious.

In Willy's case, however, the opportunity is never taken: the play does not dramatize the protagonist's "progression to enlightment" (Jackson 17). Instead of using the knowledge offered by his regressive episodes to achieve what George S. Klein terms "active reversal," Willy relies on commodity psychology to repress the conflicts anew: he clings to the American-dream myths and fantasies he used to deny and submerge the conflicts in the first place. Thus, when his pleasant picture of his sons' adoration is interrupted by his memory of Biff's misconduct, he defines the boy's behavior as spiritedness, which, we may recall, is the basis upon which Willy believes socioeconomic success is founded: "There's nothing the matter with [Biff]! . . . He's got spirit, personality. . . . Loaded with it. Loaded!" (34; act 1). Similarly, when self-doubt about his parenting interrupts his vision of showing off his boys for Ben, he imagines receiving Ben's reassurance that he was raising them to be "outstanding, manly chaps" (46; act 1), perfectly suited to fulfill their father's dreams of success. And when the memory of his refusal to accept an outdoor job from Ben interrupts his vision of receiving the job offer, Willy remembers Biff's Ebbets Field game—evidence that Biff had what it takes to be a success in Willy's competitive world and that he had therefore made the right decision in turning down Ben's offer.

Even Willy's fourth regressive episode, in which he relives the unhappy time young Biff discovered him in a Boston hotel room with another woman (102–14; act 2), does not "ope[n] the salesman's eyes" (Szondi 23) and force him to recognize "his own responsibility for what has happened to his family" (Welland 47), for the protagonist refuses to accept the painful awakening this regression offers him. As Willy recalls, young Biff flunked his high-school math course and rushed off to Boston to ask his father to pressure the math teacher into giving him the four points he needed to pass. As Bernard later explains to Willy, Biff was ready to make up the credit in summer school, if he had to, so that he could go to college in the fall. It wasn't until Biff's ill-fated trip to see his father that he gave up on his own future. Although Bernard doesn't give Willy this information until later in act 2, it is clear in the fourth regression that Willy's knowledge of his role in Biff's failure is the repressed conflict that is erupting here. When Biff first arrived at Willy's hotel room he was very eager for his father to talk to the math teacher:

"If he saw the kind of man you are, and you just talked to him in your way," Biff told his father, "I'm sure he'd come through for me" (111; act 2). It wasn't until Willy's lover came laughing out of the bathroom in her slip—and Biff realized that his father was having an affair—that the boy stubbornly refused to carry out any of Willy's plans for him. Willy represses his awareness of his role in Biff's difficulties, however, telling himself that Biff's flunking the math course is the source of his son's problems, an excuse he uses even when the adult Bernard confronts him with the truth. It is noteworthy that Willy's awareness of the importance of the hotel incident is itself an attempt to sidestep the real issue: his failure as a parent in general. As Biff later admits, his father had so raised his expectations of success—and provided so little real basis for them—that, because instant success didn't come his way, he "stole [himself] out of every good job since high school" (124; act 2). Willy's immediate flight from the restaurant where this regression occurs, to buy seeds for the plot of sterile land behind his house—an obvious escape into a time before the hotel episode occurred—underscores his repression of the psychological insight this regression provides.

It is part of the nature of conflict, however, that repression merely increases its force. Therefore, Willy's conflicts get more out of control with every attempt he makes to deny and resubmerge them. In this context, his decision to kill himself, which occurs during his fifth and final regression at the end of act 2 (119–20, 127–29), is not "an act of affirmation" (Heyen 50), nor an effort to "re-establish his own self-confidence and his family's integrity" (Moss 24), nor, as many critics would have it, a misguided attempt to secure his son's future.[7] Rather, Willy's suicide is his ultimate act of denial. Having bought the seeds he'd run off from the restaurant to get earlier that evening, Willy is now pacing off a garden plot in his backyard. It is noteworthy that planting the garden is an abstract act—not linked, like his behaviors in past regressions, to some significant, specific past event—because Willy wants to avoid the eruptions of repressed content that occurred during his more specific regressions. Unable to face the day's accumulated disappointments, he frantically seeks a way out of his despair, and commodity psychology provides one: he will kill himself in a way that appears to be an accident—in a car wreck—and Biff will collect twenty thousand dollars in life insurance. With this financial backing, Willy reasons, Biff will achieve the business success of which he believes him capable. In both segments of this regression, Willy imagines himself discussing his idea with Ben, and the deeper motive for Willy's intended suicide quickly surfaces: he wants to regain Biff's esteem so that he can regain, in his son's eyes, the personal image that used to impress the boy so much. As Willy tells Ben,

> This [Willy's death] . . . changes all the aspects. Because he thinks I'm nothing, see, and so he spites me. But the funeral—*Straightening up*: Ben, that funeral will be massive! They'll come from Maine, Massachusetts, Vermont, New Hampshire! . . . that boy will be thunder-struck, Ben, because he never realized—I am known . . . and he'll see it with his eyes once and for all. (119–20; act 2)

The blunt revelations and accusations with which Biff interrupts his father's imaginary conversation with Ben—Biff's claims that Willy raised him to be the thief he is and that he and Happy, like their father, are failures who lie about their success—seem to have no lasting effect on Willy. The only thing the protagonist takes from this experience is the fact that Biff cries to him, that Biff loves him. "That boy . . . is going to be magnificent!" (126; act 2) is Willy's final response to his interaction with Biff, and he returns immediately, his suicide project unchanged, to his conversation with Ben.

"Can you imagine that magnificence with twenty thousand dollars in his pocket?" Willy asks Ben during the second half of his final regression (128; act 2). This vision of Biff holds such charm for Willy, as does every success Biff has ever had, because Willy feels it is his own success he is experiencing in Biff's success. This is something other than healthy parental pride in a son who makes good, pride in one's success as a father—Charley's pride in his son, not Willy's, is of this kind. Willy's pride is projection, a very personal and intense form of vicarious experience. And if he can just keep this vision intact until he kills himself, Willy will not have to face the repressed awareness of his failed life that keeps threatening to break through into his consciousness and overwhelm him. Thus, the protagonist's self-destruction is a last-ditch act of repression; the twenty thousand dollars in life-insurance money intended for Biff provides both his excuse for killing himself and the fantasy he needs in order to keep self-knowledge at bay until he can accomplish it. The conflicts that constitute his psyche have come to such an impasse that ordinary forms of denial and avoidance are nothing but ineffective stopgap measures. The only way to shut *this* psyche off is to kill it. Like all his other defenses, Willy's suicide draws on the same American dream in which personal and financial success are at once wed in and transcended by sign-exchange value. For as we have seen, Willy's suicide is grounded in his vision of the increased status a showy funeral and a life-insurance legacy will purchase for him in the eyes of Biff, who has long been the repository of his father's sign-exchange value.

The play's psychological and political dimensions are fused even more clearly in the Loman family's sexuality. As Walter Davis puts it, human sexuality is primarily a matter of meanings (*Inwardness and Existence* 80–87 and passim): through one's sexuality one enacts one's conscious and unconscious attitudes and motives toward others and thereby reveals, as Merleau-Ponty put it, one's "manner of being towards the world" (158). In the Lomans' case, not only are the family's sexual attitudes compatible with the commodifying ideology of the American dream, but, like that dream, the family's sexual mores help them disguise and deny their own psychology and thereby avoid existential inwardness. In order to see how the Lomans' apparently diverse sexual natures achieve a single, ideologically saturated psychological end, we must first briefly review some key elements in the sexual characterization of each family member.

To begin with, Willy's extramarital affair, a natural focal point for any consideration of his sexuality, reveals neither "the hollowness of [Willy's] affection for Linda" (Aarnes 96), nor his unhappiness over "his failure to impress her" (Hayman 51), nor the paucity of Linda's comprehension of Willy (B. Parker). For the source of the protagonist's infidelity cannot be circumscribed by his relationship to his wife but lies in the merger of his sexual and professional identities. As we can see in the following scene, Willy's memory of his inadequacy in business is replaced by the memory of his lover:

> **Willy** [to Linda]: . . . I get so lonely—especially when business is bad and there's nobody to talk to. I get the feeling that I'll never sell anything again, that I won't make a living for you, or a business, a business for the boys. . . . *The Woman primps at the "mirror."* There's so much I want to make for—
> **The Woman**: Me? You didn't make me, Willy. I picked you.
> **Willy**, *pleased*: You picked me?
> **The Woman**: . . . I've been sitting at that desk watching all the salesmen go by, day in, day out. But you've got such a sense of humor, and we do have such a good time together, don't we?
> **Willy**: Sure, sure. *He takes her in his arms.* Why do you have to go now? (31–32; act 1)

Clearly, Willy's strong positive response to The Woman was elicited by her preference for him over the other salesmen who came through her office. Finally, someone in the business world liked him better than his competitors. For Willy, this woman was a commodity the acquisition of which conferred upon him the professional sign-exchange value he was unable to attain otherwise.

For Happy as well, women are commodities used to boost his sign-exchange value. He is not, as Brian Parker suggests, "compulsively competitive in sex and business for no reason at all" (102). Happy uses women to make him feel that he is able to "get" something that he cannot get from his career. Because he covets the attention his father has always lavished on Biff, Happy has invested a good deal of his identity in following in Willy's footsteps, in achieving the business success his father desired for both boys. Happy lives in the town in which he grew up and works in sales: he's one of two assistants to the assistant buyer for a local firm. However, although he makes enough money to support his apartment, car, and social life, he has not achieved the big success—the wealth, power, and prestigious title—that Willy's dreams had reserved for his sons. Therefore, Happy feels disappointed, cheated: a world in which he must take orders from men he "can outbox, outrun, and outlift" (17; act 1) is, he feels, an unjust world. For this reason, he compulsively seduces the fiancées of executives in his firm: he can't have their jobs, so he'll have their women.[8] We can see the connection between Happy's feelings of inadequacy in business and his womanizing when he tells Biff about his struggle to compete with his coworkers and follows immediately with, "But take those two we had tonight. Weren't they gorgeous creatures?" (18; act 1).

For both Willy and Happy, the achievement of financial success is tied to masculine self-image. This is why, as is typical in America, their metaphors for success involve winning fights and killing opponents. "Knocked 'em cold in Providence, slaughtered 'em in Boston," Willy tells his young sons upon returning home from a sales trip (27; act 1), using the same kind of language his brother Ben had used in advising him to go to Alaska: "Screw on your fists and you can fight for a fortune up there" (78; act 2). This link between business success and masculinity is, of course, one reason why both men use women to assuage their egos, to make up for their disappointments in the business world. It is no mere coincidence, then, that Happy abandons his father in the restaurant to pursue women directly upon learning that the plan for a Loman Brothers sporting-goods company is down the drain.

Of course, Happy's sexual pattern has strong Oedipal overtones as well. Raised within a family dynamic in which all Dad's attention was focused on Biff, who was an authority figure for the younger child, it is no wonder that Happy's struggle for identity and recognition early took the form of masculine competitiveness. "I lost weight, Pop, you notice?" (44; act 1) is this character's pathetic boyhood refrain as he undertakes the impossible task of competing with his-brother-the-football-hero for paternal esteem. While Willy frequently embraces Biff, in flashback as in the present, he never touches Happy. And the younger brother must listen to Dad's continual boasting about Biff without ever himself being the object of his father's pride. Happy is, thus, the perpetual bench warmer, the onlooker at the lives of his father and brother, just as Willy had been before him.

The mother's neglect of the younger son adds insult to injury and fans the flame of an already unhealthy Oedipal situation. While Linda frequently addresses Biff using the same language and tone she uses to address Willy—"I know dear" (47; act 1), "Please, dear" (59; act 1), "Thanks, darling" (69; act 2)—she uses such terms for Happy only to express contempt: "You never asked, my dear!" she responds angrily to Happy's remark that he was unaware of his father's demotion to straight commission work (50; act 1). Indeed, Happy barely exists for his mother. She frequently acts as if he were not there, as we see when the brothers return home after the restaurant scene. Although Happy does all of the talking as he and Biff enter the house, Linda ignores him to vent her emotion on Biff: "Linda, *cutting Happy off, violently to Biff*: 'Don't you care whether he lives or dies?'" (116; act 2). Only Biff's feelings matter. Only Biff's behavior can change anything. "I'm gonna get married, Mom" (61; act 1) is Happy's new hopeless bid for attention and approval. And it is in his attitude toward marriage and women that we find his Oedipal symptomatology most clearly expressed.

Happy's compulsion to seduce the fiancées of executives he works with is a rather obvious enactment of his Oedipal desire: he wants to compete with his father and brother and, especially, punish his mother for ignoring him. For Happy is a psychologically castrated man who has to use his penis to assert his existence and value. The executives he works with are, like his father and brother, authority figures. They're wealthier and more successful than he is and each has won the (symbolically) exclusive attention of a woman. He can't compete with these men in the marketplace anymore than he could compete with Biff and Willy in the home. So he punishes them by "ruining" their fiancées.

Happy can't find a girl "with resistance," a girl "like Mom" (19; act 1) that he could marry, because he doesn't want to. By sticking to his pattern of one "easy" woman after another, he can continue to fulfill two conflicting Oedipal needs simultaneously: he can continue, symbolically, to preserve his mother (no woman can take her place), and he can continue, symbolically, to soil her (to seduce a woman is to seduce his mother).

There is in Biff's psyche, as in his brother's, an important Oedipal layer. However, for young Biff, the Oedipal object was not Linda but Willy, and the relationship between father and son was a symbiotic one: each fulfilled the other's narcissistic and masturbatory phallic projection. For Willy, Biff was, of course, the star athlete, admired by the boys and pursued by the girls, as Willy had never been. For Biff, Willy was the successful businessman, universally respected and given "red-carpet treatment" by everyone everywhere he went, as Biff looked forward to being when the time came for him to take his place in the business world. Father and son saw in each other, and became for each other, an idealized phallus.

The love that bound these two characters resembled that of lovers rather than that of father and son. Linda's reminiscence with Biff certainly sounds like a description of sweethearts: "How you used to talk to him on the phone every night! How lonely he was till he could come home to you!" (51; act 1). Similarly, when Linda reminds young Biff, during Willy's flashback, that there is a cellar full of boys waiting for him, her son responds, "Ah, when Pop comes home they can wait!" (28; act 1). Biff put his father ahead of his pals, as most seventeen-year-old boys put their girlfriends. In fact, Biff put his father ahead of—or in place of—his girlfriends as well. For it was not the young girls Biff dated who received his chivalrous attentions: as we saw earlier, Biff treated the girls too roughly. As Willy's Ebbett's Field flashback reveals, it was Willy who basked in the warmth of Biff's courtly love:

> Willy: What do they say about you in school, now that they made you captain?
> Happy: There's a crowd of girls behind him every time the classes change.
> Biff, *taking Willy's hand*: This Saturday, Pop, this Saturday—just for you, I'm going to break through for a touchdown.
> Happy: You're supposed to pass.
> Biff: I'm takin' one play for Pop. You watch me, Pop, and when I take off my helmet, that means I'm breakin' out. (25; act 1)

It was Willy's hand that Biff took, ignoring Happy's comment about the girls at school (Willy's hopeless rivals for Biff's attention), and it was to Willy that Biff dedicated a special touchdown. Thus, when Biff found his father in a Boston hotel room with another woman, it was not his mother's betrayal for which the boy suffered, it was his own. Willy and Biff, in fact, sounded as if they were having a lovers' quarrel:

> **Biff,** *his weeping breaking from him:* Dad . . .
> **Willy,** *infected by it:* Oh, my boy . . .
> **Biff:** Dad . . .
> **Willy:** She's nothing to me, Biff. I was lonely, I was terribly lonely. . . . *grabbing for Biff.* . . .
> **Biff:** Don't touch me, you—liar!
> **Willy:** Apologize for that!
> **Biff:** You fake! You phony little fake! You fake! *Overcome, he turns quickly and weeping fully goes out with his suitcase. Willy is left on the floor on his knees.* (114; act 2)

Biff's outrage at Willy's betrayal of Linda—"You—you gave her Mama's stockings!" (114; act 1)—was a displacement of his outrage at Willy's betrayal of himself, Biff. So deep was Biff's hurt and anger, his sense of personal betrayal, that he rejected the relationship with his father the two had enjoyed until this point. That is, he rejected both his own and Willy's role as idealized phallus. This does not mean, however, that Biff evolved into a delayed Oedipal relationship with his mother. Psychologically, the young man could not free himself of the idealized image of Willy that had always bolstered his own narcissistic identity—he couldn't "kill" the father—and this is why Biff, unable to wholly reject the paternal belief that business success is the only success, has remained vaguely dissatisfied with the outdoor ranch life he loves.

Finally, Linda's sexuality, like her dreams for the family's future, belongs rather to her husband than herself. She is the devoted, sexless wife that "good" women were required to be in the patriarchal society of her time and place; she is the woman, as we saw Happy put it earlier, "with resistance" (19; act 1). Even her frequent use of "dear" and "darling" in addressing her husband bespeaks a motherly, rather than wifely, affection. For as we have seen, she frequently addresses Biff using the same language and tone she uses to address Willy. This is the same motherly caretaking that shows itself in her concern over Biff's remembering to take his comb to his interview with Bill Oliver and over Willy's remembering to take his glasses, handkerchief, and saccharine to his interview with Howard Wagner. Given the dearth of sexual content in Linda's behavior throughout the play,[9] the similarity of her dialogue with her husband and her older son does not suggest the eroticization of her relationship with Biff but the desexualization of her marital discourse.

The Lomans' sexual attitudes intersect in what is known in common parlance as the "good girl/bad girl" view of women. "Good girls" are virgins until marriage; therefore, they are the girls men marry. "Bad girls" do not confine their sexual activity to marriage; therefore, they are the girls men sleep with, hold in contempt, and sooner or later abandon. Obviously, the salesman and his sons enact this attitude in their talk about and behavior toward women. And Linda, who is herself a "good girl" and who calls the women Happy sleeps with his "lousy rotten whores" (117; act 2), certainly concurs with this classification system. The obvious premise underlying "good girl/bad girl" is that sex is "dirty" or evil and that women are marriage commodities whose exchange value is measured by their willingness to put their sexuality in the hands of men. Part of achieving the American dream, from this perspective, must include marriage to a "good girl" like Linda Loman, the kind of girl Willy dreams his sons will bring home—and the kind of girl Happy and Biff are unable to find. This is the pre-1960s sexual attitude associated with the social and political conservatism of post–World War II America, and clearly, it served the patriarchal status quo by maintaining male domination over women physically and psychologically. However, the "good girl/bad girl" classification supports a conservative status quo in a subtler and more powerful manner as well: it masks the psychosexual structures informing relations between the sexes and, in so doing, masks the merger of the psychosexual structures of human consciousness with the ideological structures of the socius.

"Good girl/bad girl" defines Linda's sexless, mindless devotion to Willy as virtue and thereby permits her to ignore her role in Willy's self-delusion and in her self-delusion about him. And "good girl/bad girl" offers the Loman men an excuse for their behavior with women without making any of them responsible for their own psychological subtexts. Their sexuality does not express "their resentment of the role society forces them to play" (Hayman 51). On the contrary, their social role provides them with the psychological escape they seek. Willy doesn't have to ask himself why he cheated on his wife; Happy doesn't have to probe too deeply into his motives for stealing other men's fiancées; Biff doesn't have to wonder why he used to be so rough with the girls who threw themselves at him in high school or why he has always been rather uninterested in women. The rationalization, as we all know, is that "bad girls" don't deserve better treatment—they probably don't even want better treatment—and it is "natural" for men to respond to them as objects to be used. By validating the Loman men's unexamined displacements—displacements of ontological insecurity, of career anxiety, of Oedipal desire, of phallic projection—"good girl/bad girl" helps keep them looking at the surface of their behavior, their motives, the meaning of their lives.

The conservative era during which *Death of a Salesman* was written and in which the play is set is directly related to the sexual attitudes expressed by the Loman family. For the repression of psychosexual awareness is a product of the same unconscious desire that informs the repression of political awareness: the desire to restrict the growth of critical thinking—thinking that examines motives and subtexts—which, as Horkheimer and Adorno were the first to observe, is always a threat to a conservative status quo. A conservative society's restriction of psychosexual awareness (which, as the history of the 1950s and 1980s illustrates, is accompanied by a policy of sexual conservatism on the part of America's political leadership) can be seen as an unconscious symbol of what that society really wants to repress: knowledge of ideology, of how the social/political/economic machinery runs. If we can be kept forever "innocent," forever ignorant of our own psychology and of the ways in which that psychology constitutes and is constituted by the sociopolitical domain, we will remain, like Willy, in childlike awe of the powers that be, forever seeking access to the realm of the chosen without ever questioning the terms on which that realm exists.

The relationship I have posited between ideology and sexuality might be termed an Althusserian interrogation of Lacan: the question isn't merely, How does psychosexual development mark the individual's programming within the symbolic order? but, How does the individual's psychosexual programming within the symbolic order reproduce the society's conditions of production? In other words, as Miller's play reveals, sexuality hasn't *become* public; it has always *been* public. As we see in the case of the Loman family, unexamined, repressive attitudes toward sexuality are part of the larger symbiotic relationship between the individual psyche and the socius, which finds its most self-destructive expression in the ideological armor of the American dream, the armor Willy has constructed to hide himself and his family from their own psychology.

Considered as a labor to avoid and deny existential possibility, *Death of a Salesman*'s psychological/ideological content—Willy's commodification of personal image, his five regressive episodes, and the Loman family's sexuality—can be seen as a kind of psychological death-work. As a concept applicable to the drama of everyday life, death can be seen as a labor we perform whenever we refuse the Nietzschean daily task of reconquering our humanity. As Walter Davis puts it,

> Insofar as we are dramatic beings defined by certain core conflicts, each day presents a task that will involve some expenditure of energy . . . either to confront or avoid oneself. We mobilize our [psychological] energies to move in one of these directions. Such energy is *bound* to interpretations (selective inattentions) and emotional patterns of behavior which define . . . our field of possible action. Life is the effort to make that situation the emergence of existential possibility. Death is the effort to protect us from same. (*Get the Guests* n.p.)

This is the real death, the most meaningful death, in *Death of a Salesman*: death seen not as an instinct or a drive but as an effort to avoid existential inwardness. From this perspective, the play's title gains added bite: the death in *Death of a Salesman* no longer refers merely to the way Willy ends his life but to the way he lives it as well.

This kind of death-work should not be wholly unfamiliar to most readers. Few of us can honestly assess our own family histories without seeing the same kind of avoidance and denial we see in Willy. And don't we ourselves regularly practice the kind of death-work that traps us, perhaps unconsciously but certainly not unwillingly, in static careers and interpersonal relationships? Ironically, I believe it's the ideological familiarity of Willy's death-work that informs many readers' blindness to it. Like Jay Gatsby, Willy Loman is a character whose sympathetic qualities are foregrounded in the criticism, while his weaknesses are often either marginalized or blamed on external forces. And the reason may be, again as in the case of Gatsby, that the protagonist's psychological/ideological project is compatible with those of his critics. As Esther Merle Jackson notes, "the story of Willy Loman" has an "intimate association with our aspirations" (8).

As Christopher Innes observes, "Brooks Atkinson's judgment [in 1947] that Willy 'represents the homely, decent, kindly virtues of middle class society'. . . was typical" of the critical response of that period (61), and it has remained representative of most of the critical response since that time. Eric Mottram, for example, believes that Willy's failure to succeed in business is based on his failure "to learn that business ethics . . . oppose the traditions he assumed were still in action: the personal ethics of honour, the patriarchal nature of a basically benevolent society and family, and neighborhood relations" (30). As Rita Di Giuseppe puts it, the protagonist can't "follow the praxis of the work ethic" because he is "too noble" (116). These critics don't seem to notice that Willy's personal ethics are, at best, very problematical. Similarly, June Schlueter and James K. Flanagan ignore the difficulties involved in any assessment of Willy's values in their apparent nostalgia for the mythical period they feel the character represents: "Surrounded by high-rise apartment buildings that deflect the sun from the backyard, Willy's little house in Brooklyn stands as a symbol of time past, when the world still had room for vegetable gardens and for salesmen who carried on their trade on the strength of a smile" (57). Harold Bloom, too, believes that Willy "is a good man, who wants only to earn and to deserve the love of his wife and of his sons" (15).

Even among those critics who see Willy's life and death as "a continual commitment to illusion" (Bigsby 120), there is a desire to romanticize this commitment. C. W. E. Bigsby, for example, views Willy's self-delusion as "an attempt to sustain a sense of personal dignity and meaning . . . in a life which seems to consist of little more than a series of contingent events" (117). Similarly, although William Heyen notes that Willy "die[s] lying" (49), he nevertheless calls the decision to commit suicide rather than face the truth about his life "an act of affirmation," a choice of "meaning over meaninglessness," because the character thus chooses, "in effect, to insist that he had lived, to defend his life as it was" (50).[10] And while Gerald Weales observes that much of Willy's behavior is geared to "keep him from questioning the assumptions that lie beneath his failure and his pretence of success" (134), he believes that the play's positive possibility lies only in the protagonist: the possibility "that the individual may finally be able to retain his integrity . . . does not lie in Biff . . . nor in the alternative suggested by Charley and Bernard. It is in Willy's vitality, in his perverse commitment to a pointless dream, in his inability simply to walk away" (135–36).

The desire to see Willy Loman in as positive a light as possible has, I think, also led some readers to distort other aspects of the play in order to support the reading they want to have of the protagonist. As a case in point, Bigsby asserts that Charley does not offer a positive alternative to Willy because Charley believes "that human concerns can play no role in business" and "boasts that his son's success had been a consequence of his own lack of concern" (121). However, Charley does not ignore the role of human concerns in business; he merely rejects the sentimentalization of business—and the trivialization of human concerns—apparent in Willy's attempt to substitute superficial personal interaction for meaningful business service and productivity. Furthermore, Charley's claim that he was an uninterested father, to which Dennis Welland also points as an example of this character's difference from Willy (42), is obviously not to be taken at face value. Charley's oft-quoted "My salvation is that I never took any interest in anything" (89; act 2) is followed immediately with his gift of fifty dollars to Willy and a job offer. Charley continually underplays his concerns—his love for Bernard, of whom he is clearly very proud, and his interest in Willy's well-being, which he shows throughout the play—but he has these concerns nonetheless. Behind the attempt to contrast Charley with Willy in this manner is, I think, the desire to canonize Willy as the repository of familial love in order to romanticize his motives. And it is the romanticization of Willy's motives that leads, for example, Bigsby to say that "Miller's portrait of Bernard—moral, hard-working, successful, attractive—is perhaps in danger of validating the dreams which Willy had for Biff" (122) without recognizing that Willy's dreams for Biff involved the *image* rather than the reality of such values.

Perhaps the most interesting critic to identify with Willy Loman's dream—and therefore to interpret the play in a way that supports the most positive reading possible of this character—is Arthur Miller himself. For Miller, Willy Loman is "a very brave spirit who cannot settle for half but must pursue his dream of himself to the end" (*Essays* 147–48). Willy is a tragic hero, Miller believes, largely because of the "tragic victory" of his death (*Essays* 146):

> Willy Loman is filled with a joy, however brokenhearted, as he approaches his end. . . . he has achieved a very powerful piece of knowledge, which is that he is loved by his son and has been embraced by him and forgiven. In this he is given his existence, so to speak—his fatherhood, for which he has always striven and which until now he could not achieve. (*Essays* 147)

Thus, although Miller sees Willy's suicide as an error in judgment—due to his obsession with Biff's financial future—the author considers the protagonist's death the result of his newly acquired knowledge concerning his relationship with his son. In addition, Miller points out, Willy has an important kind of *self*-awareness—he is aware "of his separation from values that endure":

> He was agonized by his awareness of being in a false position, so constantly haunted by the hollowness of all he had placed his faith in, so aware, in short, that he must somehow be filled in his spirit or fly apart, that he staked his very life on the ultimate assertion. That he had not the intellectual fluency to verbalize his situation is not the same thing as saying that he lacked awareness, even an overly intensified consciousness that the life he had made was without form and inner meaning. (*Essays* 148)

Miller is, I think, correct both about Willy's realization of Biff's love and about the protagonist's awareness of the emptiness in his own spiritual life. However, in both cases, the knowledge Willy achieves dissimulates, both for the character and for his creator, the knowledge he refuses. While Loman does realize that his son loves him, this new knowledge is, as I think I have shown, but a veneer, a gloss Willy uses to avoid and deny a deeper and much more important knowledge concerning his own psychology and that of his family. Similarly, while Willy is aware of the hollowness of his values, this is a knowledge he doesn't want to have. As I have argued, this is an awareness he struggles to repress throughout the play. In fact, it is apparently only Willy's failure to achieve even a modicum of the success he desired for himself and his family that permitted this awareness to come to the surface to begin with. Had Willy achieved any sort of material success—for example, had he been allowed to work in New York, for however little salary—and had Biff had any sort of a steady job with a future, even a job like Happy's, Willy would have been able to continue to repress his awareness of the emptiness of his spiritual life. Perhaps he wouldn't even have found it empty had circumstances allowed him to continue to hope or fantasize or lie about the future.

Miller confesses to his own unawareness of such subtextual elements in the play:

> When I saw the devasting force with which [*Death of a Salesman*] struck its audiences, something within me was shocked and put off. I had thought of myself as rather an optimistic man. I looked at what I had

wrought and was forced to wonder whether I knew myself at all if this play which I had written half in laughter and joy, was as morose and as utterly sad as its audiences found it. (*Essays* 152)

And the playwright describes his experience of artistic creation in terms that suggest the importance of the author's unconscious in the creation of a literary work: "Writing in that form was like moving through a corridor in a dream" (*Essays* 13). The form to which Miller refers is, of course, the almost exclusive use of Willy's very subjective point of view with its focus on the expressionistic memory sequences; and it is apparently this form, which Miller had never used before and would never use again, that produced the dreamlike creative experience so conducive to unconscious production. His retrospective, a year after the play's opening, confirms the notion that something other than the playwright's conscious intention went into the composition of the work: "It may well be that from the moment I read it to my wife and two friends . . . the play cut itself off from me in a way that is incomprehensible. . . . the script suddenly seemed a record of a madness I had passed through, something I ought not admit to at all, let alone read aloud or have produced on the stage" (*Essays* 12).

That Miller is not consciously aware—and, perhaps, does not want to be aware—of the powerful subtext of his play that I have outlined in this chapter is also evident in his use of setting and in the Requiem with which the play closes. For both devices bespeak an attempt to limit his audience's response to the protagonist to a much narrower reading than the play, as a whole, permits. This attempt is especially clear in the stage directions Miller includes at the beginning of the play:

> *A melody is heard, played upon a flute. It is small and fine, telling of grass and trees and the horizon. The curtain rises.*
>
> *Before us is the Salesman's house. We are aware of towering, angular shapes behind it, surrounding it on all sides. Only the blue light of the sky falls upon the house and forestage; the surrounding area shows an angry glow of orange. As more light appears, we see a solid vault of apartment houses around the small, fragile-seeming home.* (5; act 1)

This description clearly foregrounds Willy's "underdog" elements: the hero has a fight on his hands, and the enemy is an overwhelming environment. If he loses the battle, it will be the fault of social forces bigger than he is.[11] And again, as the curtain falls over Willy's grave, setting reinforces the author's message: *"Only the music of the flute is left on the darkening stage as over the house the hard towers of the apartment buildings rise into sharp focus"* (133; Requiem).

This view of Willy as a tiny boat on a big sea is reinforced by Charley's well-known speech about Willy during the Requiem. Because the other characters simply reiterate the points of view they've held throughout the play—Biff's insistence on telling the truth, Happy's refusal to acknowledge that truth, and Linda's blind devotion to her husband—Charley's apparent change of heart has marked dramatic impact:

> Nobody dast blame this man. You don't understand: Willy was a salesman. And for a salesman, there is no rock bottom to the life. . . . He's a man way out there in the blue, riding on a smile and a shoeshine. And when they start not smiling back—that's an earthquake. And then you get yourself a couple of spots on your hat, and you're finished. Nobody dast blame this man. A salesman is got to dream, boy. It comes with the territory. (132; Requiem)

Certainly, Charley's comments at this point in the play contradict his earlier view of Willy as a stubborn, foolish man, a salesman who doesn't even know what he can and can't sell (90; act 2). Neil Carson notes, in fact, that Charley's "inconsisten[t] . . . justification for Willy's romantic hopefulness" helps make the Requiem "something of a dramatic *non sequitur*" (57). Why does Miller put such unexpected words in Charley's mouth? Welland believes the explanation is that Charley "doesn't allow his feelings to come through" until Willy's funeral (42). I think, however, that these are Miller's feelings coming through rather than Charley's.

While I certainly agree that Willy is an underdog, I think that Miller uses the setting and the Requiem, not just to make this point, but to cut off other interpretive possibilities. That is, the author focuses on those elements in the protagonist's environment, both at home and at work, that can explain Willy's behavior without recourse to the kind of psychological/ideological subtext revealed, for example, in the regressive episodes. And this focus can be seen, I think, as a diversionary tactic that works to disallow the kind of reading of the play I have offered in this chapter.

It is especially interesting, in this context, to note what seems to be an incongruity in Miller's stage directions at the end of act 2. During the present-tense, realist action of the play, the actors are instructed to observe the set's predrawn wall lines, which indicate the physical boundaries among different rooms and between the house and the yard. When the actors walk through a wall line, it is an indication that they are portraying action occurring in Willy's memory of the past. These are the expressionist episodes of the play, associated with memory, fantasy, dream, imagination, and, as I have argued, regression. Yet as Linda, Charley, Biff, and Happy prepare, just before the Requiem, to go to the cemetery for Willy's funeral, they all *"move toward the audience, through the wall-line of the kitchen"* (130; act 2). Although the Requiem is supposed to take place in real time, as part of the realism of the play's present-tense action, the actors enter the scene through the wall line as if they were entering one of the play's expressionist episodes. Even if Miller deliberately violated the wall line at this point in the play—for example, as an emblem of what has happened to the house of Loman—such an intention would not undermine the unconscious symbolism of this act. Because, as we saw Miller himself suggest, the expressionist episodes are largely a product of the author's unconscious mind, it is especially meaningful that an expressionist stage direction occurs during the realist representation that ushers in the Requiem. And I think it suggests that Miller unconsciously knows the Requiem is a fantasy, his fantasy, in which he, himself, guarantees that Willy dies a tragic hero. Although Miller puts the words in Charley's mouth, it is the playwright himself, who is telling us that "nobody dast blame this man."

Thus, just like many of his critics, Miller romanticizes Willy. Or perhaps more to the point, the author mythologizes him, as Willy himself does, focusing, in Barthes's terms, on the surface of reality, or the appearance of meaning, rather than on its subtext, or the meaning of appearances (143). Perhaps, again like his critics, the author mythologizes his protagonist's psychological/ideological project out of a desire to mythologize a similar project of his own. It is a testimony to the power of the form, then, and to the power of the playwright's conflicted unconscious this form tapped, that the play tells the truth about commodity psychology and the American dream despite the desire of Miller and his critics to hide it.

4

Subject as Commodity Sign

Existential Interiority on Trial in Thomas Pynchon's *Crying of Lot 49*

Can existential subjectivity still constitute itself once the individual and the socius are symbiotically dissolved in the self-emptying commodity signs that constitute the contemporary American dream? This is the question posed by Thomas Pynchon's second novel, *The Crying of Lot 49* (1966). While Lily Bart, Jay Gatsby, and Willy Loman are finally able to escape existential inwardness only through death, in *Lot 49* the escape from existential interiority is a cultural fait accompli, and the possibility of its reconstruction is put on trial.

Protagonist Oedipa Maas, as her name implies, is on the Lacanian Oedipal cusp between the Symbolic and Imaginary orders. Upon leaving Kinneret-Among-the-Pines—a California housing development where she has lived a one-dimensional life of Tupperware and fondue parties with her husband, Wendell "Mucho" Maas—she leaves behind the flat but stable referents that have defined her existence, and now she must find new ones. In San Narciso, where she goes to execute the will of her former lover, corporate entrepreneur Pierce Inverarity, and later in San Francisco, where she spends the night wandering alone, her experiences echo Kerouac's *On the Road*, with a twist: the America that she discovers has become a proliferation of self-emptying commodity signs circulating in an endless profusion that anticipates Jean Baudrillard's notion of simulacra and Umberto Eco's concept of the hyperreal. These signs—which sell themselves as fetishized abstractions, nonthreatening substitutes for, and thus protection against, existential experience—are cultural productions, offspring of the American dream, and the novel is organized around Oedipa's desperate attempt to decipher them so that she can know, not only the culture in which she lives, but her own subjectivity as well.

In direct contrast to the minor characters' flight from existential inwardness, the protagonist becomes increasingly existentially aware and engaged over the course of the novel, seeking an alternative both to the American wasteland propagated by such corporate moguls as Pierce Inverarity and to the self-dissolution that is the minor characters' response to it. To this end, she searches for clues about the Tristero, which she believes is an organized, underground resistance mounted by the socioeconomically disenfranchised and the culturally marginalized against the dominant cultural mode of excess, artifice, and "spiritual poverty" (128) of Inverarity's America. Oedipa sees, in increasing numbers, what she believes are signs of the Tristero's existence, but she cannot be sure whether or not she is solipsistically assigning them the significance she believes they have. At the novel's close, she awaits the clue she hopes will tell her whether there "was some Tristero beyond the appearance of . . . America, or . . . just America" (137), whether the evidence she has found to support the existence of an underground resistance is real or imaginary.

Like Oedipa's desire to make sense of her semiotic world, most critics' response to *Lot 49* is also organized around the attempt to decipher the profusion of cultural signs the protagonist encounters. And despite the variety and ingenuity of that response, most analyses are informed by some version of one of the binary options Oedipa sets for herself: either there is a Tristero conspiracy or Oedipa is imagining it; either there is some transcendent meaning behind the signs of our existence or there are only the signs; either social reality can be known or we are lost in our own solipsistic indeterminacy. Perhaps Thomas Schaub presents this argument most succinctly:

> At the end of the book the questions remain: is the Tristero pattern of Oedipa's own weaving, imposed on the world outside? or is Tristero a pattern which inheres in the world outside, imposing itself upon her? Neither she nor the reader is allowed by Pynchon to ascertain the stable meaning of the blossoming pattern; and without this certainty her usefulness in preserving order against a declining culture remains painfully ambiguous. . . . Indeed, *The Crying of Lot 49* may be read as a tragic account of the difficulty of human action in a world whose meanings are always *either* our own, *or* just beyond our reach. (58–59)[1]

These options, however, rest on yet another binary opposition: that of psyche and socius. If, as in the previous chapters, we replace the dualistic view of psyche and socius informing most readings of this novel with a dialectical model of subjectivity, a third option for interpreting Oedipa's vision of contemporary America becomes possible: there is no Tristero conspiracy in America—no organized, underground resistance rooted in the underclass—but neither is she hallucinating what she takes to be the signs of its existence.

Because psyche and socius are mutually constitutive—micro- and macroproducts of the same spiritual condition—the signs of that condition automatically proliferate throughout the culture. No group need put them there deliberately. Thus, the increasing number of Tristero signs Oedipa sees over the course of the novel—the muted post horns, the WASTE and DEATH acronyms—are signs, not of a deliberate, organized conspiracy, but of the mute alienation, waste, and death that are, in one sense, the signs of America's underclass and, in another sense, the signs of an increasing entropy that is rapidly paralyzing the whole of American culture. Unless, after the narrative ends, Oedipa can begin to think beyond the binary limits of her dualistic vision of psyche and socius, she will remain, despite her existential engagement, epistemologically paralyzed by the either/or dilemma in which she finds herself at the novel's close, unable to answer her question concerning the options for the individual within contemporary American culture because she is unable to formulate adequately the concept of psyche and socius upon which such a question necessarily rests. In such a state of paralysis, she will remain unable to take action, which means she will be unable to assume a full-blown existential subjectivity, for in existential terms, we are what we do. Thus, *Lot 49* suggests that the fear of solipsism is the way that consciousness undoes both itself and its awareness of cultural reality. For the opposition of solipsism and objectivity keeps both ontology and epistemolology in the realm of the abstract and, therefore, outside history.

Given Oedipa's existential engagement, would an understanding of the dialectical relationship of psyche and socius—which would take her beyond the binary limits of her epistemology—be sufficient to inaugurate the fully realized, existential subjectivity for which she seems primed? Or is the postmodern America revealed in *Lot 49* too overwhelming a burden for existential subjectivity to bear? That is, has the symbiotic desire of psyche and socius to escape existential interiority finally created a self-perpetuating culture of emptiness that has closed down alternative ways of being? This chapter will suggest that *Lot 49* can be read as an attempt to discover the terms upon which an existentially authentic subjectivity might still be constituted in a culture grounded in the collective desire to escape existential inwardness, and it will argue that, given the America portrayed in *Lot 49*, such an attempt constitutes a nascent politics of despair, a testing of the psychological/ideological means by which one can authentically continue to explore possible alternatives to an apparently hopeless and exitless situation.

That the America portrayed in *Lot 49* is indeed based upon the collective desire to escape existential inwardness is immediately evident in the similar rendering of setting and minor characters. Setting is presented as a profusion of empty commodity signs, signs that mark an absence rather than a presence—an absence of art, of history, of myth—and therefore require no existential engagement. These avatars of the commodity psychology promoted by the American dream are "safe," emotionally insulating, nonthreatening. In Kinneret-Among-the-Pines, for example, art has been reduced to commodified pop music—exploited by a radio station that panders to "all the fraudulent dream of teenage appetites" (6)—and to the Muzak at the supermarket, which imitates, in absurd form, one of the classics: a Vivaldi concerto played on kazoos. That is, art is utterly commercialized and trivialized. It is deprived of its power and thus of its existential capacity to move us. Art is converted into an empty sign, an abstraction, a signifier that valorizes the absence of the object signified by putting a nonthreatening substitute, a commodity sign, in its place. WKCUF's teenaged listeners don't have to prove themselves by having the experiences narrated in their music; they can "prove" themselves simply by annexing the music as part of their personal sign system. Adult supermarket shoppers don't have to risk the emotions that might be engaged by the depth and breadth of a classical orchestra, or educate themselves enough to appreciate one, in order to show that they are cultured; kazoos will fill the bill just fine, thank you. Even the town's name is an empty sign: Kinneret-Among-the-Pines evokes the idea of woodlands, presumably the woodlands that were removed in order to build the suburbs of which Kinneret is a part.

In San Narciso, the city built and owned by Pierce Inverarity, empty commodity signs proliferate in even greater profusion. At Echo Courts, the motel at which Oedipa stays, the thirty-foot, sheet-metal nymph out front, with "a concealed blower system that kept [her] gauze chiton in constant agitation, revealing enormous vermillion-tipped breasts and long pink thighs at each flap . . . smiling a lipsticked and public smile" (15), is the empty sign of empty sex, the perfect wet dream of the existentially disengaged: an artificial woodland nymph on the outside and an artificial whore underneath. Yoyodyne, a giant aerospace plant, complete with barbed wire and guard towers, denies and disguises its ominous function by painting its buildings pink, the empty sign of what is usually considered the mark of the patriarchal girl child: castrated, passive, nonthreatening, and perversely seductive. The utterly artificial Fangoso Lagoons, one of Inverarity's housing projects, boasts an "ogived and verdigrised, Art Nouveau reconstruction of some European pleasure-casino" (37)—an imitation of an imitation—and a manmade lake with human bones at the bottom for scuba enthusiasts. Like every other empty commodity-sign in the novel, this one, too, offers a nonthreatening abstraction in the place of an authentic experience: buyers can simply purchase the signs of "old money" and high adventure. In order to achieve this American dream, they don't have to be anything or do anything but sign a check. As Jean Baudrillard puts it—seventeen years after the publication of *Lot 49*—Western culture is no longer concerned with imitation: "It is rather a question of substituting signs of the real for the real itself, that is, an operation to deter every real process by its operational double . . . which provides all the signs of the real and *short-circuits all its vicissitudes*" (*Simulations* 4, my emphasis).

Characterization also suggests that postmodern American culture is based on the collective desire to escape existential inwardness through simulation. Most of the minor characters have an existential experience, if not awareness, against which they are trying to defend themselves, and that defense constitutes their characterization. Indeed, the minor characters could be said to outline an architecture of commodity psychology by illustrating the kinds of avoidance behaviors facilitated by commodity culture, behaviors that, more or less, form a continuum from Mucho's successful flight from existential inwardness to Dr. Hilarius's failed attempt to escape it. The existential experience Mucho wants to avoid is that pressed upon him by the used car lot. Metzger wants protection against the existential contingencies underscored by the failed promises of his career as Baby Igor and by his insights into the convoluted nature of his own subjectivity as a former actor turned lawyer who still "acts," that is simulates, in front of a jury. Miles wants to escape his boring identity as an ordinary, American high-school drop-out working in a dead-end job. Roseman wants to deny his sense of inadequacy as a lawyer, a sense of inadequacy that reveals itself in his envious, obsessional hatred of Perry Mason. Hilarius wants to escape his past as a Nazi doctor at Buchenwald. For these reasons, each character tries to dissolve his subjectivity into the proliferation of empty commodity signs constituting the contemporary American dream. Each grounds his subjectivity in a constellation of signs that have emptied themselves by proliferating at levels of greater and greater abstraction, becoming surfaces without interiors.

"A constellation of empty signs" might be one way to define the parodic quality of each character. It could be argued that a parody is an abstraction the exaggerated quality of which derives from its constitution as an exterior without an interior, as a constellation of empty signs. Mucho is, by the novel's close, a parody of a disk jockey, groovin' to Muzak and LSD. Metzger is a parody of a Hollywood "personality," a narcissistic shell devoted to developing the capital returns of image creation/exploitation. Miles is a parody of a British rock-and-roll star. Roseman is a parody of a lawyer. Hilarius is a parody of a psychiatrist. Certainly, the socius, because it is a proliferation of empty commodity signs, in effect invites these characters to flee existential interiority in just this manner, but they all eagerly accept the invitation. Thus, America doesn't "necessitat[e] the insanity of its citizens if they are to survive in a meaningful way" (Kharpertian 106); rather, it offers them the means to do what they want to do: escape from meaning into meaninglessness.

In order to see just how the flight from existential inwardness is facilitated by a culture in which empty commodity signs proliferate, it might be helpful to take a closer look at the two minor characters whose desire for emotional insulation is most evident: Mucho Maas, whose investment in empty commodity signs allows him to finally escape his interiority, and Dr. Hilarius, whose failure to find a similar means results in his failure to escape the existential inwardness he flees.

As we learn in the novel's opening pages, Mucho has remained semiotically overloaded by the used-car lot at which he'd worked for a couple of years. All the signs he associates with the car lot are "full": they carry a heavy affective load and engage him psychologically on a level that puts his own being, the meaning of his life, at issue. Mucho had to quit that job "on the pallid, roaring arterial" (5) of a California freeway because he couldn't handle the existential inwardness pressed upon him by the interplay of two sign systems associated with that occupation: the sign system that associated the cars with the poverty and despair of their owners and the sign system that associated Mucho with those who exploited that poverty and despair by continually selling their customers "new" self-images that were nothing but the same old images recycled. For Mucho, the cars were the incarnation of the lives of people "poorer than him . . . extensions of themselves, of their families and what their whole lives must be like":

> frame cockeyed, rusty underneath, fender repainted in a shade just off enough to depress the value . . . inside smelling hopelessly of children, supermarket booze, two, sometimes three generations of cigarette smokers . . . trading stamps, . . . butts, tooth-shy combs, help-wanted ads . . . rags of old underwear or dresses . . . for wiping your own breath off the inside of a windshield with so you could see whatever it was, a movie, a woman or car you coveted, a cop who might pull you over just for drill, all the bits and pieces coated uniformly, like a salad of despair, in a gray dressing of ash, condensed exhaust, dust, body wastes. (4–5)

What really sent Mucho over the edge, however, was not the hopeless lives the cars represented—in time, "the unvarying gray sickness" might have "immunized[d] him"—but the attitude of the owners who came to trade in their cars, unaware of their own collusion with the socioeconomic system in which they were marginalized: "He could . . . never accept the way each owner, each shadow, filed in only to exchange a dented, malfunctioning version of himself for another, just as futureless, automotive projection of somebody else's life. As if it were the most natural thing. To Mucho it was horrible. Endless, convoluted incest" (5). Thus, Mucho's dismay is not just a humanitarian compassion for the plight of the poor but the terrifying belief—though never articulated as such—that subjectivity is constituted by the sign systems that make up the landscape at the site of the intersection of subject and socius. That is, he responds to a postmodern perception with existential anxiety.

We see this anxiety operating in his attempts to defend himself against the subjectivity that the semiotic landscape of the used-car lot seemed to press on him: "He shaved his upperlip every morning . . . to remove any remotest breath of a moustache . . . bought all natural-shoulder suits, then went to a tailor to have the lapels made yet more abnormally narrow, on his hair used only water" (4). The mere sight of sawdust or mention of honey—ingredients used to disguise an old car's malfunctions—"distressed him" (4). It is not merely that Mucho was afraid to be associated with the used-car charlatans who exploited the poor; he was afraid of actually *becoming* one of these people, afraid that his subjectivity would be absorbed into the sign system that, through his understated dress and grooming—a different sign system—he was trying so hard to avoid. Only such a Heideggerian anxiety, anxiety about his very being, could produce the kind of paranoia that made Mucho walk "out of a party one night because somebody used the word 'cream-puff,' it seemed maliciously, in his hearing. The man was a refugee Hungarian pastry cook talking shop, but there was your Mucho: thin-skinned" (4). The wonderful humor of this passage notwithstanding, Mucho's hypersensitivity to the mention of "all things viscous" that could be used "to ooze dishonest into gaps between piston and cylinder wall" (4) as well as the "alarming" persistence of his used-car memories (5), bespeaks an existential anxiety.

Mucho's current job as a disk jockey for a small radio station is yet another attempt to defend himself against the insights he associates with the used-car lot. Although his cynicism about his new profession makes him feel guilty—he "suffered regular crises of conscience" about it—the fact that he doesn't "believe in any of it" (3) gives him a feeling of distance and the illusion that he is somehow insulated from the semiotic world that still threatens him. Oedipa "suspected the disc jockey spot . . . was a way of letting the Top 200, and even the news copy that came jabbering out of the machine . . . be a buffer between him and that lot" (6). Thus, Mucho uses the proliferation of empty commodity signs to guard himself against the existential inwardness created by his experience of full, psychologically engaging signs. And his continual arguments with the program director concerning his image on the air function like Heideggerian "idle talk" to displace and mask deeper anxieties about issues of being.

Mucho's flight from existential inwardness reaches its greatest level of manic avoidance toward the end of the novel, when Oedipa finds him reporting for his radio station from the scene of Dr. Hilarius's shooting spree. As the program director tells her, "Day by day, Wendell is less himself and more generic. He enters a staff meeting and the room is suddenly full of people, you know? He's a walking assembly of man" (104). That is, Mucho is beginning to resemble Pierce Inverarity in his accumulation, not of multiple personalities, but of multiple personae, of multiple facades disconnected from one another and disconnected from any interior whatsoever. In fact, the very purpose of these multiple personae is to avoid interiority altogether. And it would seem that Mucho's purpose is achieved: "Mucho came downstairs carrying his [news] copy, a serenity about him she'd never seen. He used to hunch his shoulders and have a rapid eyeblink rate, and both now were gone" (105). The sense that this new serenity betokens an absence of existential inwardness is reinforced by Mucho's description of the nightmare he has finally managed to escape:

> "The bad dream that I used to have all the time, about the car lot, remember that? I could never even tell you about it. But I can now. It doesn't bother me any more. It was only that sign in the lot, that's what scared me. In the dream I'd be going about a normal day's business and suddenly, with no warning, there'd be the sign. We were a member of the National Automobile Dealers' Association. N.A.D.A. Just this creaking metal sign that said nada, nada, against the blue sky. I used to wake up hollering." (107)

Clearly, Mucho's flight is an attempt to escape his own existential insights into the nothingness of contemporary American culture and his role in that culture. That his psychological escape is facilitated by his use of drugs does not alter the meaning of that escape: he continues to take the drugs because they provide what he has long desired and been unable to provide himself. As he tells Oedipa, "You don't get addicted. It's not like you're some hophead. You take it because it's good" (107). And it is especially noteworthy that the drugs do not send Mucho off into some imaginary limbo or fantasyland; they simply focus him entirely on the cultural productions—the empty commodity signs—that already surround him.

> "It's extraordinary," said Mucho. . . . "Listen." She heard nothing unusual. "There are seventeen violins on that cut," Mucho said, "and one of them—I can't tell where he was because it's monaural here, damn." It dawned on her that he was talking about the Muzak. It had been seeping in, in its subliminal, unidentifiable way since they'd entered the place. (105)

Just as the ideology of the American dream furnishes Willy Loman with the ideological armor he uses to ward off an existential inwardness pressed upon him by his failures, so the empty commodity signs of the

American dream furnish Mucho with a psychological buffer against his existential experience of contemporary American culture, giving him an external site upon which to focus and quite literally lose himself. Paradoxically, postmodern American culture both horrifies Mucho and offers him the means by which he can escape his awareness of that horror.

While Dr. Hilarius, Oedipa's psychiatrist, shares Mucho's desire to flee existential inwardness, he does not have Mucho's apparent success in accomplishing his goal. Just as Mucho is a parody of a disk jockey, Hilarius is a parody of a psychiatrist: he tries to heal patients by making faces at them, and when Oedipa tells him she thinks she's hallucinating, he quickly says, "Don't describe it" (7). Oedipa doesn't trust him, although she continues to see him professionally, because he wants her to participate in an LSD experiment, and she's afraid he might have put some of the drug in her tranquilizers, which she therefore won't take. Nevertheless, Hilarius is probably right that Oedipa is addicted to him. As she puts it, "it's easier to stay" (8) with her psychiatrist than to leave. Of course, Oedipa's addiction to psychotherapy underscores the existential nature of her leaving Kinneret, and her therapist, for parts unknown. But it also suggests that Hilarius is aware of the potentially negative outcomes of psychotherapy. In addition, he admits that he wouldn't know when and if Oedipa were "cured," that is, ready to leave therapy. Thus, his making faces and his LSD experiments can be viewed as signs of desperation in the face of the indeterminacies of the psychoanalytic profession; and his self-abstraction as a parody of a psychiatrist is, in this context, an attempt to escape the existential inwardness pressed upon him by those indeterminacies, the existential inwardness that resulted from his guilty past as a Nazi psychiatrist at Buchenwald.

The relationship between Hilarius's psychoanalytic theory and his desire to escape his Nazi past becomes painfully, if humorously, evident when he locks himself in his office in a paranoid attempt to defend himself against Israeli retribution for that past. While he claims to have followed Freud, to have "submit[ted] [him]self to . . . the ghost of that cantankerous Jew" as a "kind of penance" (100) for having been a Nazi, it is clear that he'd hoped to find in Freud's theories an escape from the horror of his own psyche as it was revealed to him through his Nazi activities:

"Part of me must have really wanted to believe . . . that the unconscious would be like any other room, once the light was let in. That the dark shapes would resolve only into toy horses and Biedermeyer furniture. That therapy could tame it after all, bring it into society with no fear of its someday reverting. I wanted to believe, despite everything my life had been." (100)

"Freud's vision of the world," Hilarius explains, "had no Buchenwalds in it. Buchenwald, according to Freud, once the light was let in, would become a soccer field, fat children would learn flower-arranging and solfeggio in the strangling rooms" (102). Thus, for Hilarius, the possibility of a Freudian cure for the individual psyche is based ultimately on the premise that the human psyche is, by nature, healthy: to understand the unconscious reasons for one's illness is to restore the psyche to its natural, healthy state. His hyperrational reduction of Freud's views clearly serves his desire to assuage his own guilty conscience because, if such a vision were true, it would mean that his own psyche, despite what he had done at Buchenwald, was fundamentally good. Thus, Hilarius's inability to escape his guilty past rests on his inability to prove, in his clinical practice, that his psychoanalytic theories are correct. His paranoid fantasy about Israeli retribution can therefore be viewed as a projection of his own guilt and vulnerability.

While Hilarius flees existential inwardness, he obviously fails to escape it; as we have seen, he remains acutely and painfully aware of existential contingency both professionally and personally. Had he used means other than Freud—say Mucho's Muzak or Metzger's Hollywood—he'd have had a better chance. As he says in response to Oedipa's request that he help her dismiss what she thinks is her fantasy about Tristero, "Cherish it! . . . What else do any of you have? Hold it tightly by its little tentacle, don't let the Freudians coax it away or the pharmacists poison it out of you. Whatever it is, hold it dear, for when you lose it you go over by that much to the others. You begin to cease to be" (103). It would seem that Hilarius is advising Oedipa to believe whatever she needs to believe in order to avoid the kind of adaptation to the contemporary American socius that results in the psychological death of many of the minor characters. Without realizing it, he is, in effect, advising her to believe in Tristero because to do so is to believe in the possibility of an alternative to Inverarity's America.

It is indeed Inverarity's America—the legacy of the corporate mogul—in which the minor characters seem to proliferate on a par with the empty commodity signs that surround them. For as Oedipa realizes near the novel's close, "San Narciso," the city built and owned by Pierce

Inverarity, "had no boundaries. . . . She had dedicated herself, weeks ago, to making sense of what Inverarity had left behind, never suspecting that the legacy was America" (134). While the American dream, a Hegelianism for the masses, rests on a view of human development as progressive, *Lot 49* shows that human development, at least in America, has begun to devolve. This is the America that unfolds through the growing awareness of Oedipa Maas.

In direct contrast to the minor characters, Oedipa moves from existential blindness and bad faith to existential awareness and engagement. In leaving Kinneret, she leaves behind a manner of being in the world (*en soi*) and being for herself (*pour soi*) that she'd hidden behind her whole life. In Kinneret,

> there had hung the sense of buffering, insulation, she had noticed the absence of an intensity, as if watching a movie, just perceptibly out of focus, that the projectionist refused to fix. And had also gently conned herself into the curious, Rapunzel-like role of a pensive girl somehow, magicallly, prisoner among the pines and salt fogs of Kinneret, looking for somebody to say hey, let down your hair. . . . it turned out to be Pierce. . . . But all that had then gone on between them had really never escaped the confinement of that tower. (10)

It is significant, then, that upon leaving Kinneret, Oedipa first experiences the kind of paranoia many of the self-dissolving minor characters experience. Once one's experience becomes existential, there are no guarantees—anything can happen. Watching television in her motel room with Metzger, coexecutor of Pierce's will and child star of the movie before them on the screen, she thinks her companion might have arranged somehow to have the film shown at her hotel room the first night they meet as part of a seduction plot. Thus begins what will become her increasing awareness of the synchronicity that marks all the narrative events and her attempt to rationally order and explain the connections she sees. The attempt, however, is doomed to failure: the phenomena she observes do not fall into discrete, rational categories but overlap and invade one another in a convoluted, multilevel manner that defies interpretation. Of course, with Oedipa's increasing frustration comes an increasing anxiety that matches or surpasses that exhibited by the minor characters. Yet the protagonist does not self-dissolve. She continues to undertake the impossible task of decoding the excess of data with which she is inundated.

Like her attempt to decode cultural signs, however, Oedipa's existential engagement is frustrated by its failure to produce concrete results. For example, following her night in San Francisco, she meets an old sailor with the d.t.'s. Her initial response is to ask, "Can I help?" (92). And, indeed, she tries to help: she holds the man in her arms, gives him money, and mails a letter for him through what she believes is the Tristero's underground postal system. But the entire incident is shot through with the hopelessness she expresses as she rocks the old man in her arms: "'I can't help,' she whispered . . . 'I can't help'" (93). Similarly, when Oedipa meets Winthrop Tremaine, the swastika salesman, a few days later, she is of course appalled by his fascist racism. She wants to do something about him, but she does nothing: "She left wondering if she should've called him something, or tried to hit him with any of a dozen surplus, heavy, blunt objects in easy reach. There had been no witnesses. Why hadn't she?" She realizes that she, that all Americans, are responsible for America—"This is America, you live in it, you let it happen" (112), she tells herself—but she takes no action.

Even her insight into the class structure in America, the only conclusion she draws about which she expresses no doubts, begins with existential engagement but issues in inaction. Having lost everyone she thought might help her—Mucho, Dr. Hilarius, Metzger, Driblette, Fallopian—Oedipa goes into a state of depression. She is, as she puts it, "saturated" (133), overloaded with signs the meanings of which she can't be certain. Hitting bottom, she becomes a mass of physical and psychological symptoms: she has headaches and "waves of nausea" (129), is disoriented, plagued by nightmares, and, as we see when she drinks and drives without headlights, suicidal. Significantly, it is in this state of mind, with an utterly existential experience of herself and her world, that Oedipa's perceptions of America are pointedly insightful. She realizes that the only true continuities in America consist of "storm systems of group suffering and need" and "prevailing winds of affluence" (134). She realizes that Pierce's great wealth and the corporate structure on which it depends are replicated throughout America, as is the underside of that world:

> She remembered now old Pullman cars, left where the money'd run out
> or the customers vanished, amid green farm flatnesses where clothes
> hung, smoke lazed out of jointed pipes. . . . She thought of other, immo-
> bilized freight cars, where the kids sat on the floor planking and sang
> back, happy as fat, whatever came over the mother's pocket radio; of

other squatters who stretched canvas for lean-tos behind smiling bill-
boards along all the highways, or slept in junkyards in the stripped
shells of wrecked Plymouths. . . . She remembered drifters she had lis-
tened to, Americans speaking their language carefully, scholarly, as if
they were in exile from somewhere else invisible yet congruent with the
cheered land she lived in; and walkers along the roads at night, zooming
in and out of your headlights without looking up, too far from any town
to have a real destination. (135)

As always, Oedipa's first response to this realization is an existentially engaged one: she wants to take action; she wants to do something
to help. She wonders, "What would the probate judge [of Pierce's es-
tate] have to say about spreading some kind of a legacy among them all,
all those nameless, maybe as a first installment?" (136). However, feeling powerless, she immediately abandons the idea: she knows the judge
would be "on her ass in a microsecond, revoke her letters testamentary,
they'd call her names [and] proclaim her through all Orange County as
a redistributionist pinko" (136). Thus, while Oedipa's existential awareness and engagement increase over the course of the novel, she never
reaches the point of taking the action that defines a full-blown existential subjectivity. And part of her inability to take action is due to an epistemological paralysis based on her binary view of her situation.

The protagonist's conception of her options—that either the Tristero
is a real, underground organization or else she is having paranoid delu-
sions about the nature of contemporary American culture—keeps her
in the same spot waiting for an answer. And she will remain on that
spot until she discovers her third option, the excluded middle: namely,
that the horror of contemporary America is exactly as she sees it
whether or not there is some Tristero giving its alienated periphery a
collective voice. In other words, Oedipa must realize that, in contemporary America, paranoia is no longer a mental illness; it is the response of
a social realist.

This is the subjectivity the final scene seems to await, just as Oedipa
awaits the Tristero. The description of the room in which the auction of
Inverarity's stamp collection (lot #49) is about to take place, and where
Oedipa awaits what she hopes will be a clue to the existence of the
Tristero, has the unmistakable ring of an existential universe:

The men inside the auction room wore black mohair and had pale, cruel
faces. They watched her come in, trying to each conceal his thoughts. . . .
Oedipa sat alone, toward the back of the room, looking at the napes of

necks, trying to guess which one was her target, her enemy, perhaps her proof. An assistant closed the heavy door on the lobby windows and the sun. She heard a lock snap shut; the sound echoed a moment. (137–138)

This passage could have come straight from Sartre's *No Exit*: hell is other people, and there is no way out; we are locked together in a sunless room, each of us in a state of utter isolation, trying to conceal our thoughts. All that is needed to complete the picture is an existential hero—a Merseult or a Roquentin. Whether or not, at some point after the narrative ends, Oedipa will take that step, whether or not she will finally take some action in keeping with her existential engagement, remains a question that raises an even more important question addressed in the novel: Is such a step still possible in contemporary America?

Can a full-blown existential subjectivity still be constituted in a land "conditioned . . . to accept any San Narciso among its most tender flesh without a reflex or a cry" (136) by a culture whose members increasingly resemble the empty commodity signs they so eagerly annex? In other words, if existential subjectivity is measured by existentially authentic action, what, in Oedipa's world, should that action be? The protagonist believes there is nothing to do but wait, "if not for another set of possibilities to replace those that" currently exist, "then at least, at the very least . . . for [the] symmetry of choices to break down, to go skew" (136). Yet what hope is there that the "symmetry of choices" Oedipa has outlined—organized alienation or madness, wealth or poverty—will, of its own accord, "break down"? The prognosis seems especially dim as these binary oppositions are apparently so firmly established: "It was now like walking among matrices of a great digital computer, the zeroes and ones twinned above, hanging like balanced mobiles right and left, ahead, thick, maybe endless" (136). Given this view of contemporary America, if *Lot 49* is a novel about the possibility of constituting an existential subjectivity in this nation today, then it must also be a novel about the politics of despair, about the ways in which one can continue to take meaningful action in a situation that is apparently hopeless and exitless. This despair is evident in the novel's overlapping social, philosophical, and psychological themes.

As Oedipa knows, "excluded middles" are "bad shit" (136), and *Lot 49*'s America is a nation of excluded middles. As we have seen, on the one hand, there is the extreme wealth of the ruling class, represented by the estate of Pierce Inverarity, for whom the American dream is the "need to possess, to alter the land, to bring new skylines, personal antagonisms, growth rates into being" (134); on the other hand, there is the extreme poverty of the homeless, "the squatters," the heirs to "300 years of . . . disinheritance" (135). Whatever middle ground there is in the novel is inhabited by such self-dissolving abstractions as Mucho, Roseman, Dr. Hilarius, Metzger, Miles, Fallopian, and Driblette, and thus that middle ground has a vanishing ontological status.

Paradoxically, in the semiotic domain, the entire cultural fabric of America is rapidly tending toward an entropic sameness that blankets the novel's landscape, denying and disguising the socioeconomic disparities of our class system much as the layer of pink paint covering Yoyodyne denies and disguises its sinister purpose. It is interesting to note that most readings of *Lot 49*'s treatment of entropy hinge on the contrast between definitions of entropy in thermodynamics—the tendency of heated molecules to disperse their energy to colder molecules until a uniform temperature, or random sameness, is achieved—and in information theory, or cybernetics, in which entropy is a measure of the amount of uncertainty in the information content of a message: the more possible meanings a message has, the more entropy, or ordered difference, it has. Thus, while an increase in thermodynamic entropy indicates an increase in sameness, an increase in information entropy, the argument goes, indicates an increase in differentiation. Theodore D. Kharpertian notes, for example, that

> in thermodynamic terms, Oedipa moves from a state of greater entropy, a condition of inactive uniformity in which her "days seemed . . . more or less identical" ([*Lot 49*] 2), to a state of lesser entropy, a condition of active diversity made possible by the apparent existence of the Tristero. In cybernetic terms, however, she moves in the opposite direction, that is, from lesser to greater entropy, as the multiplicity of information she gathers about the Tristero increases the uncertainty of the information's ultimate significance. *The Crying of Lot 49* depicts, therefore, the cybernetic evolution of Oedipa from a condition of unknowledgeable certainty to one of knowledgeable uncertainty. (104)

In cultural terms, then, as Dean A. Ward notes, Oedipa moves from a uniform, univocal, suburban America to an America characterized by infinite multiplicity, an America where anything can happen and where events can have any number of meanings (26–29).[2]

However, in the postmodern world of *Lot 49*, information theory's traditional model, which is used to oppose cybernetic entropy to thermodynamic entropy,

INFORMATION SENT	NOISE	INFORMATION RECEIVED
A +	N =	A or B or C or . . .

Source: Adapted from Shannon and Weaver (5).

no longer obtains. According to this model, an original message (A) can, at least theoretically, be determined, against which received versions (A or B or C or . . .) could be measured. The model thus relies on the possibility of a stable, knowable original message. In *Lot 49* there is no such possibility. Therefore, uncertainty becomes, not just a function of choosing among numerous possible received messages, but a function of never knowing, even theoretically, that any original message ever existed. Perhaps none of the received messages is the "correct" one. Or perhaps the noise itself is the real "message." Information in *Lot 49* has thus reached a new plateau: all messages could mean anything; therefore all messages are, in effect, the same—unknowable. In this context, information entropy and thermodynamic entropy lead in the same direction: the more information entropy, or uncertainty, increases, the more all messages become the same. Castillo's definition of entropy in Pynchon's short story "Entropy" reinforces the collapse of thermodynamic and information entropy in *Lot 49*. He describes it as a "tendency from the least to the most probable, from differentiation to sameness, from ordered individuality to a kind of chaos" (74). In the novel, then, entropy in either domain leads to sameness, diminished energy, and death.

Sameness, diminished energy, and death are, as revealed by the minor characters' flight from existential inwardness, desiderata in the world of *Lot 49*. As Mucho happily explains, when he tells Oedipa about his newly acquired ability to process sound without the aid of electronic devices,

"No matter who's talking the different power spectra are the same, give or take a small percentage. . . . Everybody who says the same words is the same person if the spectra are the same only they happen differently in time, you dig? But the time is arbitrary. You pick your zero point anywhere you want, that way you can shuffle each person's time line sideways till they all coincide." (106)

Just as the novel's architectural landscape—the endlessly repeated freeways and suburbs, the innumerable Fangoso Lagoons and Echo Courts and Yoyodynes—melts together in the ultimate coincidence of simulation, so Mucho wants to merge with "a million lives" (107) and thereby lose himself. This is the same "fascination with senseless repetition" that haunts Jean Baudrillard's *America* (1) and Umberto Eco's *Travels in Hyperreality*. However, Pynchon suggests that the desire at work here, the desire for what Eco calls "the Absolute Fake," is not, as Eco asserts, the "offspring of the unhappy awareness of a present without depth" (31). Rather, it is the *desire for* a present without depth. In other words, *Lot 49* indicates that the desire informing the flat postmodern landscape—Nature obliterated to make room for Fangoso Lagoons, in which natural objects are artificially reproduced—is the same desire informing the flat postmodern psyche. It is psychological entropy—sameness, diminished energy, and death—that finally makes Mucho's face "smooth, amiable, at peace" (106).

This desire for psychological entropy, for existential insulation, is underscored by the contrast between the dry descriptions of sexual desire, which isolates rather than bonds participants, and the much more passionate descriptions of the desire for emotional insulation. The sexual passes the male characters make at Oedipa are perfunctory, consisting of brief verbal games that the men apparently don't even expect to succeed. That is, sexual passes are social, rather than passional, in nature. The only sexual encounter described in the novel is that between Metzger and Oedipa at Echo Courts, and this interchange, too, is impersonal, shot through with the two characters' mutual isolation.

The encounter begins, tellingly, with Metzger "fast asleep with a hardon" (26). When he awakes to Oedipa's kisses, she falls asleep, both metaphorically—she is "so weak she couldn't help him undress her" (26)—and literally: "it took him 20 minutes" to undress her, and "she may have fallen asleep once or twice" (26). Furthermore, as Metzger undresses her, he reminds Oedipa of "some scaled-up, short-haired, power-faced little girl with a Barbie doll" (26). When Oedipa "aw[akes] at last to find herself getting laid," she responds by "count[ing] each electronic voice" she hears in the "fugue of guitars" coming from out-side the window (26–27). Thus, Oedipa is passive, psychologically ab-sent, and Metzger is turned on, not by sex, but by power, a fact that is reinforced by his subsequent elopement with a fifteen-year-old girl. The lovers' isolation is underscored by the song with which the Paranoids serenade the pair, a love song in which the following words, in the fol-lowing order, dominate: *lonely, lonely, still and faceless moon, ghost, shadow, gray, alone, alone, lonely, lonely, lonely, gray, dark, alone, lonely, lonely*. Finally, when Oedipa and Metzger achieve climax, "every light in the place . . . go[es] *out, dead, black*" (27, my emphasis). Yet this "love scene" is not presented as a disappointment to either character; indeed, it initiates their liaison.

In sharp contrast to the tone of impersonality and isolation that in-forms the portrayal of sexual desire, the desire for existential insulation is described in passionate, sensual terms. During Oedipa's all-nighter in San Francisco, she has an experience that helps explain why the mi-nor characters are drawn to the protection against existential inward-ness afforded by self-dissolution. At one point during her wandering, the protagonist, perhaps because of her "linearly fading drunkeness" (86), feels that she has become invulnerable, beyond the reach of the dangers associated with night in the street, that is, beyond existential contingency:

> The city was hers, as, made up and sleeked so with the customary words and images (cosmopolitan, culture, cable cars) it had not been before: she had safe-passage tonight. . . . Nothing of the night's could touch her; nothing did. . . . *She was meant to remember.* She faced that possibility as she might the toy street from a high balcony, roller-coaster ride, feeding-time among the beasts in a zoo—any death-wish that can be consum-mated by some minimum gesture. She touched the edge of its voluptuous field, knowing it would be lovely beyond dreams simply to submit to it; that not gravity's pull, laws of ballistics, feral ravening, promised more delight. She tested it, shivering: I am meant to remem-ber. Each clue that comes is *supposed* to have its own clarity, its fine chances for permanence. (86–87)

Note the sexually charged nature of the language in this passage: *made up, sleeked, roller-coaster ride, consummated, voluptuous, lovely beyond dreams, submit, delight, shivering*. What Oedipa finds so attractive here is the psychological death, the release from existential contingency and responsibility, that results from believing that all things occur that are meant to occur; that she, like everything else, is merely fulfilling a purpose imposed from the outside; that she is not responsible. This release—the release from existential interiority—not sex, is the big turn-on.

That the constitution of an existential subjectivity in Pynchon's America requires a politics of despair is also evident in the novel's representation of our limited epistemological resources. Indeed, most critics note the importance of uncertainty or indeterminacy for our understanding of the novel.[3] Yet I don't think that *Lot 49* invites us to "celebrate . . . our absolute inability to know" (Olsen 162). Rather, it illustrates the ways in which our "paradigms determine what we perceive" (Palmeri 980). Thus, at least in terms of my own paradigm of the dialectical symbiosis of psyche and socius, Oedipa can't make cultural meaning out of all the cultural data she accumulates because she limits herself to explaining it in terms of some sort of conspiracy theory that implicitly separates the individual and the society into discrete entities. For example, it occurs to her that Inverarity might have set up, as an elaborate hoax, the innumerable "clues" she has found in support of the Tristero's existence. And she believes that if this is not the case, then the signs of alienation she sees everywhere—the muted post horn is the most ubiquitous example—are either placed there by an organized underground or are products of her imagination. What she doesn't realize is that, because psyche and socius are dialectically related in a mutually constitutive symbiosis, cultural meaning is diffused through all layers of culture. There is no conspiracy in the usual sense of the word, just the synchronicity—the innumerable connections, doublings, coincidences—that results from the unconscious, pervasive, collective desire that saturates, constitutes, and reflects cultural reality at any given moment. Because cultural meaning saturates all agents and objects, it is constantly "announcing" itself, constantly producing the connections that would make one suspect a conspiracy in the first place.

The interconnectedness of all cultural phenomena is responsible for Oedipa's recurrent observation of what she believes are hieroglyphs. She repeatedly senses, as she gazes on some typical American scene, that she is looking at a hieroglyph that holds the key to some revelation. For example, her first view of San Narciso reminds her of a printed circuit, like those found in transistor radios:

The ordered swirl of houses and streets, from this high angle, sprang at her now with the same unexpected, astonishing clarity as the circuit card had. . . . there were to both outward patterns a hieroglyphic sense of concealed meaning, of an intent to communicate. There'd seemed no limit to what the printed circuit could have told her (if she had tried to find out). . . . she and the Chevy seemed parked at the centre of an odd, religious instant. As if, on some other frequency, or out of the eye of some whirlwind rotating too slow for her heated skin even to feel the centrifugal coolness of, words were being spoken. (13)

And indeed, San Narciso—like Fangoso Lagoons, the L.A. freeway, and all the other cultural phenomena that seem to Oedipa to carry messages—is a hieroglyph that can communicate any number of insights into contemporary America. All the cultural phenomena in the novel are, in fact, hieroglyphs for one another because they are all manifestations of the same supersaturated solution that automatically diffuses its meaning, as a solution diffuses its molecules, throughout its material existence.

This synchronicity of cultural phenomena is emblematic of the interface of psyche and socius because it suggests that we are all conspiring, albeit for the most part unconsciously, in whatever occurs in the socius. Because of these innumerable interconnections, the path of all inquiry, which is unavoidably grounded in the culture of the inquirer, leads, albeit circuitously, back to itself, back to the question and the questioner with which it began, just as Oedipa's night-watch in San Francisco both begins and ends at John Nefastis's house. She doesn't find an objective answer to her question about the Tristero on her labyrinthine pilgrimage to the heart of postmodern America because knowledge, at least knowledge about the nature of one's socius, consists of what one is able to articulate of one's diffusion within it, not of "objective" answers to "objective" questions.

Indeed, one of the novel's most successful projects is to undermine the belief in objectivity—the New Critical epistemology—that, at the time of the novel's publication, had dominated academia for over two decades. Oedipa goes to see *The Courier's Tragedy*, a ficticious play by a fictitious seventeenth-century playwright, Richard Wharfinger, hoping to find a clue to the Tristero, to which she thinks the drama may allude. Driblette, the director, explains that a text exists not in the words on paper, not as a New Critical, autonomous object that remains stable and inviolate over time, but in the mind of the creator of any particular version of that object, that is, in the mind of the interpreter. Driblette thus implicitly calls for what is now termed reader-response theory: texts tell us not about themselves nor about their authors but about ourselves. Any act of interpretation that conceives of itself as a transparent, ahistorical, objective apprehension of words on paper—the text in itself—is as absurd and impossible an activity as the attempt to establish authorial intention. Both yield nothing. As Driblette tells Oedipa,

> "You know where that play exists, not in that file cabinet, not in any paperback you're looking for, but—" [his] hand . . . indicate[d] his . . . head—"in here. . . . The words, who cares? They're rote noises to hold line bashes with, to get past the bone barriers around an actor's memory, right? But the reality is in *this* head. Mine. . . . You could fall in love with me, you can talk to my shrink, you can hide a tape recorder in my bedroom, see what I talk about from wherever I am when I sleep. . . . You can put together clues, develop a thesis, or several, about why characters reacted to the Trystero possibility the way they did, why the assassins came on, why the black costumes. You could waste your life that way and never touch the truth. Wharfinger supplied words and a yarn. I gave them life. That's it." (56)

The only real conspiracy in the novel, then, is that of the author to confound any attempt—Oedipa's or ours—to make New Critical sense of the narrative events. The novel abounds in minor characters who remain little more than names dashing in and out, never to be heard from again, and with fictional historical trivia too numerous to be tied into an organic whole. Pynchon overloads us with data we can't possibly process or even keep track of without laborious note taking that doesn't repay our effort. Thus, while *Lot 49* raises the questions that narrative generally raises—Which events are central to the plot and which are peripheral? What is the significance of any given event in terms of the text as a whole? What does the text as a whole mean?—the novel frustrates our attempts to answer them. In so doing, *Lot 49* foregrounds the desires involved in our wanting those questions answered and in our attempts to answer them. The novel thus suggests, as does reader-response theory, that our epistemologies are grounded in our desires and that the power of reading lies, in large part, in our willingness to become self-reflexive about the activities in which reading engages us.

This view of cultural meaning as nonobjective, as a diffusion in which psyche and socius are mutually implicated, is underscored by the text's references to "Bordando el Manto Terrestre," a painting by Spanish exile Remedios Varo. Oedipa remembers seeing the painting during a trip to Mexico with Pierce Inverarity some years ago. It consists of

> a number of frail girls with heartshaped faces, huge eyes, spun-gold hair, prisoners in the top room of a circular tower, embroidering a kind of tapestry which spilled out the slit windows and into a void, seeking hopelessly to fill the void: for all the other buildings and creatures, all the waves, ships and forests of the earth were contained in this tapestry, and the tapestry was the world. (10)

That is, the tapestry the girls are creating is also the tapestry within which their tower is contained. Thus, all reality is at once personal and cultural, the product of a personal projection that both creates and is created by the socius. The two cannot be meaningfully separated, and any question about the one always implies a question about the other. Without a dialectical conception of their relationship, Oedipa's attempts to understand her culture and her place within it will remain mired in the epistemological limitations that lead her to the despair she experiences at the novel's close. However, there is no guarantee that a dialectical understanding of psyche and socius will significantly lessen that despair because, while such an understanding provides a holistic sense of psychosocial reality and the only meaningful place to begin inquiry, by its very nature it does not offer the kind of psychological assurances—epistemological closure, certainty, mastery—we have come to rely on.

Finding no sure answers in contemporary reality, Oedipa turns to history for an explanation that will help her make sense of her world and herself, that will lift her out of her growing desperation. Specifically, she looks for clues to the development of the Tristero from its origin in seventeenth-century Europe to its establishment and growth in America. With the help of scholar Emory Bortz, the protagonist tries to determine the original text of *The Courier's Tragedy*, collates references to the Tristero in various editions of the play, gathers data on the dramatist's life as well as on the historical period during which the play was written and first performed, and consults "obscure philatelic journals" (119) that might contain information about the Tristero's history. By this point the Tristero has become, not just an underground communication network for America's alienated or even the European underground postal system that it began as, but an emblem of the possibility of knowing anything. As it turns out, however, history's indeterminacy makes a politics of despair only more unavoidable.

Despite Oedipa's diligence in tracking down clues and the college training that seems to have suited her well for just such tedious scholarship, she keeps running into blind alleys. "Beyond its origins, the libraries told her nothing more about Tristero," and Bortz's educated speculations were useless, merely "a species of cute game" (122). Given the impossibility of acquiring sure knowledge about the events occurring in the immediate vicinity of the perceiver, how can sure knowledge possibly be gained about events from which the perceiver is separated by both time and space? Indeed, Oedipa realizes the impossibility of determining historical causes for trivial and important events alike:

> Did she know why Driblette had put in [his production of *The Courier's Tragedy*] those two extra lines [referring to the Tristero] that night? Had *he* even known why? No one could begin to trace it. A hundred hangups, permuted, combined—sex, money, illness, despair with the history of his time and place, who knew. Changing the script had no clearer motive than his suicide. (121)

She becomes angry when Mike Fallopian tells her to separate fact from speculation—"Write down what you can't deny. Your hard intelligence. But then write down what you've only speculated, assumed. See what you've got" (126)—because she knows that speculation is just about all she's got. As Bortz and his graduate students point out when Oedipa asks them for historical data concerning the author of *The Courier's Tragedy*, "The historical Shakespeare. . . . The historical Marx. The historical Jesus. . . . they're dead. What's left? Words" (113). In short, "historical figuration" is nothing but a seductive scam consisting of "breakaway gowns, net bras, jeweled garters and G-strings . . . layered dense" (36) over a proliferation of historical events rendered virtually unknowable by their complexity, as well as by their temporal distance from us.

Perhaps the best metaphor for the complexity of historical events, both past and current, and for the impossibility of acquiring any kind of complete knowledge of them, can be found in the can of hair-spray that takes flight in Oedipa's bathroom at Echo Courts. The passage begins with Oedipa looking in the bathroom mirror, itself a metaphor for the desire to comprehend or establish her identity, which, as we have seen, is part of what she seeks in seeking to understand postmodern America. Rather tipsy from drinking Beaujolais with Metzger, Oedipa

> fell over, taking a can of hair spray on the sink with her. The can hit the floor, something broke, and with a great outsurge of pressure the stuff commenced atomizing, propelling the can swiftly about the bathroom. . . . The can . . . bounced off the toilet and . . . continued its high-speed caroming. . . . the . . . wild, flashing over-flights of the can . . . seemed inexhaustible. . . . The can knew where it was going, she sensed, or something fast enough, God or a digital machine, might have computed in advance the complex web of its travel; but she wasn't fast enough, and knew only that it might hit them at any moment, at whatever clip it was doing, a hundred miles an hour. . . . The can collided with a mirror and bounced away, leaving a silvery, reticulated bloom of glass to hang a second before it all fell jingling into the sink; zoomed over to the enclosed shower, where it crashed into and totally destroyed a panel of frosted glass; thence around the three tile walls, up to the ceiling, past the light . . . amid its own whoosh and the buzzing, distorted uproar from the TV set. (22–23)

Almost all the qualities imputed to the runaway hair-spray can in this passage—its high speed; the practical impossibility of predicting or even mapping the trajectory of its "complex web"; the destruction left in its wake; the distinction between "its own whoosh" and the "distorted uproar" of the television in the next room, that is, of the media that pretend to report such news events—provide a model that illuminates the concept of history informing the whole novel. While history in *Lot 49* isn't a function of total ontological chaos, it creates total epistemological chaos. History is a system of spiraling connections and reactions that bounce in any given direction for any given distance and at any given speed for any number of reasons: obstacles encountered, angle of impact, speed of impact, and so on. History is thus a function of factors too numerous and complex to grasp with any degree of certainty.

It is significant that the hair-spray can shatters the mirror into which Oedipa is looking when the scene begins, for the breaking of the mirror betokens the relationship between history and yet another avatar of the necessity for a politics of despair: nostalgia for the Lacanian Imaginary order. Lacan's Imaginary order, which dominates early childhood, is initiated and informed by what he calls the mirror stage, when our subjectivity is reflected back to us—through other people if not through literal mirrors—as a stable unity.[4] It is this sense of our self and our world that is shattered by the Lacanian Symbolic order or, put more simply if not more precisely, by history. For our initiation into the Symbolic order, because it is an initiation into our culture as it is inscribed in language, is intrinsically historical. As we have seen, Oedipa's initiation into postmodern American culture is the novel's pervasive theme. And it's an initiation she resists as much as pursues, because she is "anxious that her revelation not expand beyond a certain point. Lest, possibly, it grow larger than she and assume her to itself" (125). Indeed, as she muses over Driblette's grave, she "wonder[s] whether . . . some version of herself hadn't vanished" (121). And this vanished version of herself is the buffered, illusory subjectivity she lived in Kinneret, before her initiation into the Symbolic order of postmodern American culture.

It is noteworthy, then, that mirrors appear at those times when Oedipa seems on the verge of yet another new and potentially threatening discovery: for example, the morning she visits her lawyer concerning her executrixship of Inverarity's will; during her first meeting with Metzger; during her first and only meeting with Driblette; the day she discovers Bortz's edition of *The Courier's Tragedy*; upon learning that WASTE, which she believes is the name of the Tristero's underground communications system, stands for We Await Silent Tristero's Empire; and just before she learns that an absentee bidder for Inverarity's collection of philatelic forgeries might be from the Tristero. Her looking in mirrors can thus be read as a desire to recapture the stable, unified version of herself she once knew or, in other words, a desire to return to the safety of the Imaginary order. The protagonist's inability to find the self-image she seeks in mirrors—"she . . . tried to find her image in the mirror and couldn't" (26); "in the mirror [she saw] [n]othing specific, only a possibility" (54)—underscores the unattainable, purely nostalgic nature of her desire.

Nostalgia for some former Edenic experience of wholeness that might be associated with the Imaginary order occurs throughout the novel in more concrete ways as well. For example, on her way to visit Fangoso Lagoons with Metzger, Oedipa muses nostalgically about the Pacific Ocean:

> Somewhere beyond the battening, urged sweep of three-bedroom
> houses rushing by their thousands across all the dark beige hills . . .
> lurked the sea, the unimaginable Pacific. . . . Oedipa had believed, long
> before leaving Kinneret, in some principle of the sea as redemption for

Southern California . . . some unvoiced idea that no matter what you did
to its edges the true Pacific stayed inviolate and integrated or assumed
the ugliness at any edge into some more general truth. (36–37)

Here we have nostalgia for Nature as the source of Truth, a source
that remains always whole and stable, "inviolate and integrated," capable of "assum[ing]" all attacks against its wholeness "into some more
general truth." This is nostalgia for Nature as the source and sign of the
Imaginary order, of a stable, unified self in a stable, unified world.

This same kind of nostalgia for a pristine, pre-Symbolic sort of subjectivity occurs during her all-night vigil in San Francisco. She wonders
if all the clues she has found in evidence of the Tristero's existence
"were only some kind of compensation. To make up for her having lost
the direct, epileptic Word, the cry that might abolish the night" (87).
This is the same "epileptic Word" she associates with some "central
truth" hovering, throughout the novel, just beyond her ken, whose
source lies in some earlier experience she cannot remember:

She could, at this stage of things, recognize signals . . . as the epileptic is
said to—an odor, color, pure piercing grace note announcing his seizure.
Afterward it is only this signal . . . and never what is revealed during the
attack, that he remembers. Oedipa wondered whether at the end of this
[journey] . . . she too might not be left with only compiled memories of
clues, announcements, intimations, but never the central truth itself,
which must somehow each time be too bright for her memory to hold. . . .
(69)

Here, again, Oedipa longs for some kind of direct, immediate access
to some "central truth" that she has somehow lost, some Edenic knowledge that would give her back to herself whole and stable.

The protagonist's haunting desire to return to some earlier, more
stable order of being underscores her inability to imagine a future in
postmodern America. And it is at this point—with all the traditional
ego supports removed—that existential subjectivity based on a politics
of despair must begin. Upon what ground is such a politics to be undertaken within the framework of this novel? That is, do we have anything
left in *Lot 49* upon which it can be built? The answer, I think, is no. We
have an American dream consisting of a profusion of empty commodity signs. We have a cast of characters who, as "death-wishful" and
"sensually fatigued" (44) as Wharfinger's seventeenth-century audience is purported to have been, dissolve their own subjectivity into

those empty commodity signs in order to flee existential inwardness. We can't be sure why this state of affairs obtains in America because contemporary culture, as well as our own history, has become little more than an overload of indeterminate data. And we have a protagonist, the only character in the novel willing or able to sustain an existential inwardness, who doesn't know what to do because she doesn't know whether or not she can trust her own perceptions.

Reading the novel in terms of a fully existentialized dialectical model of subjectivity suggests that Oedipa does not attain the heroic stature some readers see in her. She does not "achieve an awareness of her culture," which, because she "maintains her ground," allows the reader to "experience . . . a sense of the possibility for meanings which inhere in the world and in language" (Schaub 67). Nor does the protagonist evolve into "a satiric heroine, attacking the republic's undifferentiated and monolithic sterility" (Kharpertian 85). Instead, she engages in an existential struggle to learn what, if any, authentic existence can be lived in the America Pynchon portrays.

While *Lot 49* thus asks if an existential subjectivity can be constituted in a postmodern culture so horrifying that our only viable response to it must be a politics of despair, the novel, in keeping with the problematic it portrays, doesn't provide an answer. Instead, the text explores the landscape of the despair in which an authentic postmodern politics—if it is to exist at all—must be grounded. In other words, if a postmodern American subject is to have an authentic politics at all, it must be a politics of despair because despair is the only existential reality left us. We are not told, however, what such a politics will do or even how such a politics can, with certainty, be recognized. If *Lot 49* tells us anything about the politics of despair, it tells us that it is a politics with no certain, stable ground on which to stand. It is a politics that asks us to look horror straight in the face with no sure hope of doing anything to change or escape it. And it is a politics that can't even tell us if we'll survive the effort. Perhaps, like Mucho, Metzger, or Miles, we'll become cultural "personae," types, empty commodity signs of a bankrupt culture. Perhaps, like Dr. Hilarius, we'll give ourselves over to hysteria. Perhaps, like Driblette, we'll commit suicide. Or perhaps, like Oedipa, we'll wait for more information, knowing, as she knows, that we're all executors of Pierce Inverarity's will yet unwilling or unable to shoulder that responsibility in some concrete way.

At what point will Oedipa's quest for the Tristero, her quest for knowledge of an alternative, become an end in itself, a function of the bad-faith desire to at once have a purpose in life yet eschew the responsibility for taking action?[5] Perhaps a politics of despair demands an existential subjectivity that will acknowledge uncertainty and take its best shot anyway, because at stake is an America whose narcissistic death wish is in danger of drowning us all in the refuse of our repressed collective psyche. For if Baudrillard is right that, in contemporary America, "death ha[s] found its ideal home" in the excesses of "a utopian dream made reality" (*America* 31, 30), then surely it is because that dream is one of empty commodity signs, whose primary psychological attraction is that they insulate us against existential inwardness, which means that they insulate us against life. If this is one of the stories *Lot 49* tells, then Oedipa's "you live in it, you let it happen" (112) is an admonition Pynchon directs at us all. Existential awareness of postmodern horror—in its apparent boundlessness and with no guarantee of any escape—may not be a sufficient response to postmodern culture, but it is, according to Pynchon, the necessary first step.

5

Beyond *Being and Nothingness*

The Corporate Commodity in
Joseph Heller's *Something Happened*

As Adam J. Sorkin observes, differences among critical commentaries on Joseph Heller's *Something Happened* (1974) have revolved around the "issue of the novel's emphasis on the pathology of personality versus the interpretation of external actuality" (36). Is Heller's second novel—a 569-page interior monologue rendered from the point of view of rising advertising executive Bob Slocum—primarily a psychological study of one individual's tortured psyche, concerned, as Richard Hauer Costa suggests, "with the forces in man which cause him to be terrified of himself" (160)? Or, given that the corporation for which Slocum works is, as Evan Carton puts it, "a synecdoche for America" (49), is *Something Happened* primarily a sociological study of the cultural forces responsible for individual pathology?[1] This chapter will attempt to show that the critical focus on this distinction misses the novel's analysis of a subtler phenomenon that obviates this debate: the protagonist's flight from existential inwardness, a psychological/ideological project the fulfillment of which collapses the boundary between the individual and the socius by merging the depersonalized/depersonalizing desire of both.

While *Something Happened* maps the psychological subsumption of the individual by the corporation for which he works, this process is not an example of corporate or national colonization of individual consciousness in which the protagonist is an unwilling or unaware victim. Nor is it, as Susan Strehle's oft-quoted Sartrean reading of the novel suggests, an existential critique of the bad faith required to accomplish the protagonist's capitulation to corporate interiority. Rather, Heller's novel examines one of the most efficient means available in contemporary American culture—corporate commodity psychology—for the individual's flight from existential inwardness, a flight whose self-aware and deliberate nature places it beyond the victim model of the relationship between the individual and the socius that informs most historically situated readings of this novel and beyond the existential problematic that informs the works analyzed in the preceding chapters.

Having succeeded, by the novel's opening, in climbing the American dream's socioeconomic ladder by commodifying his personal image according to corporate standards, Heller's protagonist uses a corporate economy as his template to commodify, and thereby try to escape, his own existential interiority. As we shall see, a consciousness commodified on the corporate model achieves the American dream—and accomplishes its flight from existential inwardness—by reducing psychological experience to the kinds of abstract relations that obtain among commodities in late capitalist culture: pleasure is reduced to sign-exchange value, to the fetishization of the signifier; nostalgia is reduced to memory commodified, in which the other becomes an abstraction incapable of impinging on one's subjectivity; sex is reduced to sign-exchange value as well, and to the masturbatory insulation it thus provides; and love is reduced to a vulnerability to existential contingency, a vulnerability that creates the kind of interiority the project was formed to eliminate. This is an inwardness that, like its corporate template, merely duplicates and coordinates external conditions, an inwardness constituted by absence: absence of pleasure, absence of relatedness, absence of the kind of desire associated with emotion, with affect. This is the postmodern inwardness that Jean Baudrillard compares to "the control screen and terminal . . . endowed with . . . the capability of regulating everything from a distance" ("Ecstasy" 128). And this is the inwardness that, at the novel's end, Slocum finally succeeds in acquiring.

As the novel opens, Slocum's ability to commodify his image in the corporate style is evident in every aspect of his social behavior. In contrast to Willy Loman, this salesman of self-image does everything right. He dresses exactly right for every occasion; he takes up the "right" sport (golf), although he doesn't enjoy it; he goes to the "right" dinner parties and invites the "right" people to his dinner parties; he expresses the "right" opinions; he sleeps with prostitutes, although he doesn't want to, when the "right" person in the company invites him to do so; et cetera ad nauseum. Slocum knows that the work he accomplishes is of peripheral importance, if any, because the company's product continues to sell and the company continues to grow without apparent effort on anyone's part. That the company and its product are never named underscores the novel's focus on the psychology of hierarchical corporate structure rather than on the psychology of industrial production. As the protagonist is well aware, the company's success, like his own, is based upon its accumulation of the *signs* of success: costly, tastefully decorated offices; well-dressed, well-paid, sophisticated employees; luxurious convention sites. Indeed, Andy Kagle, longtime head of the Sales Department, finally loses his job to Slocum largely because the protagonist's dress and manners are more refined, more in keeping with the image of sophisticated success the company wants to promote.

Slocum's perfectly constructed exterior—calm, cool, rational, in total command of himself and of his immediate environment—covers, however, an interior that is besieged by every conceivable fear and barely in control of itself or of anything else. Slocum lives in terror of aging, death, illness, and accidents, both for himself and for his family, and he obsessively imagines an endless variety of catastrophes that could occur. He is afraid that his wife might commit adultery, that he might become sexually impotent, that his son might grow up to be homosexual, that his young daughter might become pregnant. He fears the dark. He fears handicapped people and authority figures. In short, he is afraid that something might happen "for which [he] could not have prepared [him]self" (6; ch. 1). The novel's intensely disturbing quality is due largely to the hellish, tortured images that constitute much of Slocum's inner world: "Things stir, roll over slowly in my mind like black eels, and drop from consciousness into inky depths. Smirking faces go about their nasty deeds and pleasures surreptitiously without confiding in me. Victims weep. No one dies. There is noiseless wailing" (398–99; ch. 6).

His fears are exacerbated by his lack of a unified or consistent ground of self-reference: Slocum feels he consists of many different "selves," some of whom he doesn't even know. He can't experience himself as a coherent and cohesive whole because his desire to be the perfect corporate commodity requires that he show each "buyer" a marketable surface. Because the only value a commodity has is that assigned to it by a purchaser, Slocum "packages" himself with false fronts in order to produce what he believes is the most desirable effect for each situation. These masquerades occur as much at home as at work, and they reveal Slocum's desire to be accepted by others without be coming emotionally engaged. Afraid of rejection and unwilling to risk pain, he pretends to have the feelings he thinks others desire. Because he behaves in this way with everyone and at all times, he doesn't know when to stop: he repeatedly finds himself imitating the speech, posture, and gestures of the person with whom he is speaking. It is no surprise, therefore, that Slocum lacks a sense of self: "I often wonder what my own true nature is. . . . The problem is that I don't know who or what I really am" (73–74; ch. 3). This feeling of self-alienation is reflected in his experiences of disconnectedness from his own body and his own behavior that occur, for example, when he "float[s] away" from conversations in which he is engaged "and begin[s] to feel [he is] looking down upon a . . . show of stuffed dolls in which someone I recognize who vaguely resembles me is one of the performers" (506; ch. 7).

Such loss-of-self experiences bespeak a fundamental confusion of Slocum's inner and outer worlds. He sees himself through the eyes of so many others that a privileged "inside," or private, perspective is lost, reduced to the fears and hostilities he is continually working to hide. Indeed, he is afraid that someday he "will blend [his] inner world with [his] outer world and be disoriented in both" because he has "trouble enough deciding which is which now and which one is the true one" (246; ch. 5). We can see inner and outer worlds merge in much of Slocum's language: he often uses metaphors of the workplace, the outer world, to describe his thoughts and feelings, his inner world, as, for example, when he speaks of people he has rejected as "dead records in [his] filing system" (104; ch. 3) or describes his relationship with his wife in terms of emotional profit and loss.

While the contrast between the exterior surface the protagonist presents to the world and his interior experience of himself may, at first, seem shockingly incongruous, these two aspects of his personality are, in fact, logically compatible: they mirror the conditions of production in his company. As an entity, the company shows a confident, placid exterior to the public, but internally, at the level Slocum occupies in the corporate hierarchy before his promotion at the novel's close, fear is the oil that lubricates operations:

> In the office in which I work there are five people of whom I am afraid. Each of these five people is afraid of four people (excluding overlaps), for a total of twenty, and each of these twenty people is afraid of six people, making a total of one hundred and twenty people who are feared by at least one person. Each of these one hundred and twenty

people is afraid of the other one hundred and nineteen, and all of these one hundred and forty-five people are afraid of the twelve men at the top who helped found and build the company and now own and direct it. (13; ch. 2)

The only way the minor executives feel safe is if everyone below them is literally their inferior. As Green puts it, "'I don't want whistlers working for me. I want drunkards, ulcers, migraines, and high blood pressure. I want people who are afraid. . . . God dammit, I want the people working for me to be worse off than I am, not better,'" (414; ch. 6). Thus, the company's signs of placid refinement are empty: like Slocum, its confident, calm exterior is constituted by signs that belie its fear-ridden interior.

Although Slocum's fears attach to many different objects—personal, familial, occupational—they have but one source: all of his frightening fantasies result from his commodity psychology, from his adoption of a corporate economy for use in the psychological domain. It's not a question of the corporation *causing* any given event or problem in the protagonist's life, but of corporate logic—the valorization of extreme competitiveness, paranoia, and sign-exchange value—informing Slocum's very way of being in the world. He relates to himself and to his family with the same fear and loathing he experiences with his co-workers, and he knows it, as we can see in the following passage in which he sardonically describes his family in the same language he used to describe his coworkers: "In the family in which I live there are four people of whom I am afraid. Three of these four people are afraid of me, and each of these three is also afraid of the other two. Only one member of the family is not afraid of any of the others, and that one is an idiot [Slocum's brain-damaged child]" (355; ch. 5).

Suspicious that his family conspires against him, Slocum is always jockeying for position, for control: "She [his wife] wants me to tell her I love her. I won't. . . . This is one advantage I have over her that I'm still able to hang on to" (520; ch. 7). He doesn't even trust *himself* outside the constraints imposed by an exterior authority:

> I wonder what kind of person would come out if I ever did erase all my inhibitions at once, what kind of being is bottled up inside me now. Would I like him? I think not. . . . Deep down inside, I might really be great. Deep down inside, I think not. I hope I never live to see the real me come out. He might say and do things that would embarrass me and plunge him into serious trouble. (248; ch. 5)

This passage reveals the anxiety that is the source of all his fears: anxiety that he cannot fit the mold his company has produced for rising executives, anxiety that he is not internally constituted for corporate success, anxiety about his own interiority. This is the inwardness Slocum feels he must vanquish. All the objects of his fear—the day-to-day events in his personal, familial, and professional life—are really Heideggerian displacements: because he is tortured by anxiety about his very being, he displaces it into fear of every possible object in his environment.[2]

Despite the Lukácsian nightmare that Slocum's adoption of corporate economy has made of his psyche, he has no desire to adopt a different template for human relations. In fact, the protagonist feels more at home at the office than he does with his family: at work the rules are official, the boss's authority is final, and everybody plays the game the same way. Of course, the game is not enjoyable; it's a torturous struggle for an uncertain and transient hegemony. But he prefers the game to the risks of personal engagement he would face if there were no masks or role playing. And if he plays it well enough, he might be promoted—he would like to become the head of an important department—and moving up the corporate ladder means everything to him. If he could just climb high enough to achieve the pinnacle of the American dream, like Arthur Baron and Horace White, Slocum believes that he would be beyond the internal struggles that make up the company at the lower levels of operations and that make up his own identity as well. He wants to constitute his interiority according to the model on which the company is constituted, but he wants to do so at the highest executive level possible, the level at which, he believes, the placid exterior the company shows to the world also constitutes its internal operations. Slocum wants to be like the men at the top: "They seem friendly, slow, and content when I come upon them in the halls (they seem dead)" (13; ch. 2). "They seem dead." Although this statement may appear to be a critique of the corporate heads, it actually reveals the secret and primary attraction of the corporate upper echelon. Slocum's desire is to be dead inside, to feel nothing, to be safe. If the corporate leaders represent, as James M. Mellard suggests, the Lacanian Symbolic order (146), then it is a Symbolic order grounded in accidie, for the object-object relations that are the emergent value in *The Great Gatsby* are the dominant value here.

Although Slocum's awareness of the utter contingency of life gives him the inwardness, and the existential opportunity, of Sartre's Roquentin, in *Something Happened* the existential project of *Nausea* is turned on its head. Roquentin's realization that all existence is tenuous and can change radically at any moment—and that the ultimate contingency is death—creates his existential engagement with life. For it is life's lack of any guarantee, and the spotlight this condition puts on issues of being, that make an existential attitude toward life possible. Given that existence is not grounded in some underlying, unchanging, timeless principle, what should I do with my life? This is the fundamental existential question and the fundamental existential opportunity because it puts all issues of being and action, of metaphysics and politics, in one and the same place: in one's own hands. Thus, an awareness of contingency is, for Roquentin, the source of the possibility of existential growth, an occasion for the assumption of personal responsibility for his being and actions.

In contrast, Slocum's awareness that life is utterly contingent, his "dread of everything unknown that may occur" (8; ch. 1), results in his obsessive desire to flee that awareness entirely. And given that the ultimate existential contingency is death, it should not be surprising that Slocum's flight into psychological death is also related to his fear of biological death.

> I think about death.
> I think about it all the time. I dwell on it. I dread it. . . . I dream about death and weave ornate fantasies about death endlessly and ironically. (And I find—God help me—that I still do want to make that three-minute speech. I *really do* yearn to be promoted to Kagle's job. Last night in bed, I stopped dwelling on death for a while and began formulating plans for either of the two speeches I might be asked to make. . . .) (343; ch. 5)

As this passage illustrates, long before Slocum achieves the accidie that characterizes his interiority at the novel's close, he uses his desire for advancement—his desire to achieve the American dream—and his obsession with the small victories and failures that make up his daily routine at the office to escape an awareness of his own mortality. Because, as we have seen, his desire for advancement is linked to his desire to be emotionally dead, this character presents us with a fascinating irony: in order to deny death, he seeks death-in-life.

It is not that the possibility of the existential project is overcome by Slocum's fear of failure; rather, according to the corporate values by which he lives, the *success* of the existential project would constitute failure. To remain existentially engaged in the contingency of being means that one has not achieved the "correct" subjectivity. Discontent can't become the occasion of a revelation and the opportunity for growth; it can only be a sign that one hasn't "fit in" the way one should. Thus, Slocum's terror of the gaze of the other—his awareness that one is continually evaluated by others—is not, as it is for Sartre, anxiety about having his inwardness, his self-representation, appropriated by others. Slocum *wants* his inwardness appropriated by the other—the corporate Other. The protagonist's attempts to escape his inwardness by commodifying it, by emptying his consciousness until it becomes merely an exterior constituted by the commodifying gaze of the corporate Other, are manifest in his lack of pleasure in the world, his sexuality, and his role in and reaction to the death of his older son.

Slocum's lack of pleasure in the world is evident in the "nothing's-any-good-anymore" refrain to which his interior monologue frequently reverts. Sex, food, and consumer products are not what they used to be, he tells us, and he doesn't even enjoy that avatar of the American dream, his home:

> All of us live now—we are very well off—in luxury . . . in a gorgeous two-story wood colonial house with white shutters on a choice country acre in Connecticut off a winding, picturesque asphalt road called Peapod Lane—and I hate it. There are rose bushes, zinnias, and chrysanthemums rooted all about, and I hate them too. I have sycamores and chestnut trees in my glade and my glen, and pots of glue in my garage. I have an electric drill with sixteen attachments I never use. Grass grows under my feet in back and in front and flowers come into bloom when they're supposed to. (Spring in our countryside smells of insect spray and horseshit.) (359; ch. 6)

Slocum doesn't hate his home because he would prefer to be somewhere else; he hates it for the same reason he hates everything. His dissatisfaction with the world is, rather obviously, a displacement of his dissatisfaction with himself. For example, when humiliated by his boss, Jack Green, Slocum thinks, "I'd like to shoot him in the head. I wish I could make a face at him and stick my tongue out. (I wish I could have a hot sweet potato again or a good ear of corn.)" (417; ch. 6). The protagonist wishes he could do something about Green, wishes he could be a "tough guy" with a gun or even a tough little boy making faces. Unable, however, to effect any change in his immediate environment, he beats a hasty retreat from confrontation and humiliation by shifting the focus of his displeasure to the problems of the larger world where, as Slocum likes to remind himself throughout the novel, nothing is as good as it used to be and nothing can be done about it. This maneuver allows him to avoid responsibility for doing something about his relationship with Green and to avoid the feeling of failure that would be engendered by an unsuccessful attempt to ameliorate his situation.

There is, however, another, more important reason behind the "nothing's-any-good-anymore" refrain: he finds no pleasure in the world because he has reduced pleasure to sign-exchange value. His acquisition of objects and annexation of accomplishments solely for the prestige they confer have made pleasure an abstraction. Thus Slocum, in a single breath, reduces his expected promotion and his sex life—both present and past—to the element they have in common, which is the only content he wants them to have: sign-exchange value.

> Who cares if I get Kagle's job or not? Or if I do get into young Jane in the Art Department's pants before Christmas or that I was never able to graduate myself into laying older-girl Virginia on the desk in the storeroom of the automobile casualty insurance company . . . ?
>
> *I* care. I want the money. I want the prestige. I want the acclaim, the congratulations. And Kagle will care. And Green will care, and Johnny Brown will care. . . . But will it matter, will it make a difference? No. Do I want it? Yes. (136; ch. 4)

The protagonist doesn't *enjoy* the object or the activity because he doesn't really interact with or participate in it: his eye is always on the status, on the abstraction. As Jean Baudrillard explains in *For a Critique of the Political Economy of the Sign*, "It is not the passion (whether of objects or subjects) for substances that speaks in fetishism [the cathexis of pleasure in an object or activity], it is the *passion for the code* which, by governing both objects and subjects, and by subordinating them to itself, delivers them up to abstract manipulation" (92). That is, what we really fetishize is not the object (not its use value, not the signified) but the signifier. Thus, "fetishism is not the sanctification of a certain object or value. . . . It is the sanctification of the system as such, of the commodity as system: it is thus contemporaneous with the generalization of exchange value and is propagated with it" (92). And if fetishism, or the sanctification of commodification, "is always invading new territories, further and further removed from the domain of economic exchange value strictly understood"—that is, if it is invading areas such as sexuality and recreation—"this is not owing to an obsession with pleasure, or a substantial desire for pleasure or free time, but to a progressive . . . systemization of these sectors" (92).

Baudrillard's observations help us understand why Slocum's ever-increasing activities—professional and recreational—and accumulation of goods are inversely proportional to his pleasure in them, why he intones the perpetual refrain, "I don't enjoy anything anymore" (325; ch. 5): he is annexing a code, a sign system, an abstraction that removes him emotionally from the objects he acquires and the activities he performs, and that collapses the private and public sectors, the personal and professional domains of his life, into a single, flat dimension governed by status, by the code, by the signifier.

Although it may seem that emotional distance is the price Slocum pays for status, it is actually part of the payoff, part of the incentive to commodify himself and others. For this character wants, at all costs, to be safe from feeling. It is here that Heller can help us extend Baudrillard's theory. For Baudrillard, the sanctification and generalization of exchange value and sign-exchange value is progressive: the problem is self-perpetuating. Heller shows us one of the reasons why this is so: commodification provides a sense of emotional safety, of psychological insulation. Thus, for Heller, Slocum finds no pleasure in the world because he doesn't want to. Lack of pleasure in the world keeps him from desiring anything and keeps him protected. His wish to desire nothing is well served by the conclusion that there is nothing worth desiring, that "there is nothing new and good under the sun" (372; ch. 6):

> Smut and weaponry are two areas in which we've improved. Everything else has gotten worse. The world is winding down. You can't get good bread anymore even in good restaurants . . . and there are fewer good restaurants. Melons don't ripen, grapes are sour. They dump sugar into chocolate candy bars because sugar is cheaper than milk. Butter tastes like the printed paper it's wrapped in. Whipped cream comes in aerosol bombs and isn't whipped and isn't cream. People serve it, people eat it. Two hundred and fifty million educated Americans will go to their graves and never know the difference. . . . That's what Paradise is— never knowing the difference. (483; ch. 6)

"Paradise is . . . never knowing the difference" because, if one never knows the difference, one never wants other than what one has.

That Slocum is willing to forgo pleasure in order to avoid pain is further evidenced by his low tolerance for anything painful or even unpleasant. He has a strong aversion to hospitals, sick people, and funerals and avoids all three; he avoids talking with his wife about her problems, just as he avoids talking to Martha, the typist in his office who is slowly going crazy, just as he pretended not to notice when his mother had a stroke. He leaves town when his family is looking for a new nurse for his severely retarded son, Derek, or when the family is moving to a new house. And he avoids his daughter's problems by avoiding any real contact with her:

> When she tells me she wishes she were dead, I tell her she will be, sooner or later. . . . When she told me, in tones of solemn importance, that she hoped to have a lover before she was eighteen and would want to live with him for several years even though she is never going to get married, I nodded approvingly and wisecracked I hoped she'd find one. . . . And when she came to me, even that first time, to say she wasn't happy, I told her that I wasn't either and that nobody ought to expect to be. By now, she is able to anticipate many of my sardonic retorts and can mimic my words before I say them. (132; ch. 4)

Unlike Harry in Faulkner's *Wild Palms*, who decides, "*Between grief and nothing, I will take grief*" (324; ch. 7), Slocum is willing to feel nothing at all in order to avoid feeling pain. When a friend dies, his sadness is always accompanied by "a marked undercurrent of relief, a release, a secret, unabashed sigh of 'Well, at least that's over with now, isn't it?'" (187; ch. 4). His lack of feeling for his wife was, he believes, one of the reasons he might have married her (195; ch. 4) because the last thing he wants is to be emotionally involved with the people he lives with:

> I keep my mouth shut and my sentiments suppressed, and I adamantly refuse to merge my feelings with hers. (I won't share my sorrows. I don't want her to have a part in them. They're all mine.) I wish I had no dependents. It does not make me feel important to know that people are dependent on me for many things. It's such a steady burden, and my resentment is larger each time I have to wait for her to stop crying and clinging to me and resume placing the silverware in the dishwasher or doing her isometric hip and thigh exercises. (I can't stand a woman who cries at anything but funerals. I feel used.) (450; ch. 6)

The only pleasure Slocum freely allows himself is nostalgia, and even here the primary attraction is the emotional safety nostalgia offers. The protagonist likes to recall the desire he had as a youth of seventeen for Virginia Markowitz, a young woman of twenty-one who worked in his office before he was drafted into the army. But he was glad to learn, on his return from the service, that she was dead, because it saved him the risk of taking her to bed, which his army uniform and his experience of the world finally made him feel he was capable of doing. And he is glad now that she is no longer alive because, he says, she would still be four years older than he and no longer attractive: "I think I am still in love with her (and glad she is dead, because otherwise I might not be, and then I would have no one)" (476; ch. 6). Slocum's tone here reflects his feelings at this moment: a combination of sarcastic self-awareness and loneliness. He is sardonically aware that he doesn't really want to have Virginia in any concrete way; he "wants" her only in fantasy. Nevertheless, this state of affairs is a lonely one. Of course, his real reason for being glad Virginia is dead is that it frees him from the possibility of emotional involvement he would have faced had she been alive. Love, then, is experienced as extreme vulnerability to contingency. In this context, nostalgia becomes the only safe way to experience love. As memory commodified, nostalgia turns the other into the perfect object: an abstraction molded to fit one's needs without making one vulnerable to another's subjectivity.

Slocum's sexuality is another revealing index of his flight from existential inwardness through corporate commodity psychology. As we saw in chapter 3, through one's sexuality one enacts one's conscious and unconscious motives and attitudes toward oneself and others. In *Something Happened*, Heller presents sexuality primarily as missed opportunities nostalgically remembered or compulsively pursued. In both instances, sexuality is commodified: sexual encounters/partners become acquisitions that embody two related desires—the desire for status and the desire for emotional insulation. Slocum's sexuality underscores his investment in both these desires. Although the protagonist has frequent sexual relations, he doesn't "get that hot anymore" (385; ch. 6). Drive-discharge, born of the need to vent the frustrations of modern living, has become, he tells us, his reason for having sex: "Apathy, boredom, restlessness, free-floating, amorphous frustration, leisure, discontent at home or at my job—these are my aphrodisiacs now" (385; ch. 6). However, if physical release were his sole motive for sexual relations, as John Aldridge believes (39), why does he need to have them so frequently and with so many different partners, especially given that he experiences only "sluggish, processed lust," which he has "to make a laborious effort to enjoy" (313; ch. 5)? The reason is that in sex, as in every other area of his life, Slocum seeks "safety and invisibility" (227; ch. 5), and through misogyny and the reduction of sexual pleasure to sign-exchange value, he achieves it.

Like Giraudoux's Paris in *La guerre de Troie n'aura pas lieu*, Slocum likes to "faire l'amour à distance" (32), make love at a distance. However, while Paris values emotional distance in his partner—it is Hélène's aloofness that excites him, not his own—Slocum values emotional distance in himself, not because he finds it stimulating, but because he finds it safe. Although sex can sometimes be physically exciting, he keeps it utterly impersonal: "I do not think of it as doing something together and don't believe anyone else really does, either" (443; ch. 6). He avoids the possibility of closeness with a woman by having many lovers and by not spending time with any one of them: "I don't want to see any of them frequently and can't bear being with them long. They want to talk afterward, get close, and I want to sleep or go home. (I like to date working girls for lunch in Red Parker's apartment because I know they'll have to leave shortly to get back to their jobs.)" (363; ch. 6). And if he is strongly attracted to a woman, he avoids getting involved with her at all, as he avoids his coworker, the "slim, smiling, tall, supple, very young Jane, a kid, my refreshing new temptation in the Art Department. . . . I move closest to Jane when there is no chance of moving closer; I never joke with her about meeting after work unless I know it's impossible" (362–63; ch. 6).

Of course, an effective way to keep sex impersonal is to treat women like objects. Therefore, Slocum likes to think of Jane as "a present I intend to give myself for Christmas this year" (154; ch. 4) and to depersonalize his lovers by thinking of them collectively, as "all [his] Pattys and Judys, Karens, Cathys, and Pennys" (362; ch. 6). As objects, their function is to please him: "Most of my girls have been very good to me" (362; ch. 6). Their function does not involve their having needs and feelings of their own: "I liked it better when they thought they were doing us a favor. I'm sorry they ever found out they could have orgasms too" (424; ch. 6). When a woman ceases to be an object for Slocum—when she expresses desires of her own—he evades the encounter by experiencing profound disgust: "That octopus of aversion had been there in bed with me and my wife again this morning when she awoke me with languorous mumbles and by snuggling close, that meaty, viscous, muscular, vascular barrier of sexual repugnance that rises at times (when she takes the initiative. It may be that I prefer to do the wanting)" (470; ch. 6). As this passage suggests, a feeling of Sartrean nausea characterizes Slocum's fundamental relationship to his wife's desire because her desire is beyond his control. Like Roquentin's epiphany before the gnarled roots of the old tree, it plunges him into the world of contingency he is continually laboring to escape. At these times, it serves his purposes well to be repelled by women's sexual organs: "They've got nothing there but something missing. I think filthy" (383; ch. 6).

Slocum usually treats women as objects by sadistically exploiting their personal weaknesses: "I feed on submissive feminine loneliness like a vulpine predator. I'm drawn by the scent" (366; ch. 6). Sexual aggression is not his "means of asserting his essential self-worth" (129), as Joan DelFattore suggests in her interesting analysis of Slocum's dream world, but his means of achieving the sense of mastery—and distance— he wants: "Generally speaking, I prefer to make *them* do all the doing and giving; that way I feel I *have* done something to them: I've gotten away with something" (366; ch. 6). For this reason, he also likes to force his wife to have sex with him against her desire, if not her will: "I like to fuck my wife when she's not in the mood. I like to make her do it when she doesn't want to" (399; ch. 6).

When he does give a woman pleasure, his motive remains selfish and sadistic; his desire is to feel important and in control, to see his partner at what he considers a disadvantage, and thereby to feel removed from her:

> Were it not for the element of status, I really would rather not give orgasms . . . and there's even an element of sadistic cruelty in [my giving them]. Some of them change so grotesquely. They *ought* to be ashamed. There really is something disillusioning and degenerate, something alarming and obscene, in the gaudy, uncovered, involuntary way they contort. It's difficult not to think lots less of them for a while afterward, sometimes twenty years. (365; ch. 6)

Slocum's misogyny is his way of keeping himself insulated and safe from the emotional connection he might otherwise feel for women with whom he is sexually involved. Because he is closest to his wife, he is in most danger with her of feeling emotionally connected. For this reason, he sets up the rules of the game to preclude the possibility of being sexually satisfied with her. He would be dissatisfied no matter how she looked: "I wish my wife had bigger tits. I wish my wife had smaller tits" (220; ch. 5). And he would be dissatisfied no matter how she performed in bed: "I'm really not sure I *want* my wife to be as lustful and compliant as one of Kagle's whores or my girl friends, although I know I am dissatisfied with her when she isn't" (125; ch. 3).

Even more effectively than misogyny, however, the reduction of sexual pleasure to sign-exchange value provides Slocum with a barrier against the emotional risks of sexual closeness. In Slocum's company, sexual activity, provided it is handled with a certain amount of savoir faire and discretion, is associated with corporate success. Male employees are expected to be sexually active—including visits to prostitutes—in and outside of marriage; even the top executives and the very old men are careful to allude to their sexual exploits at the company's annual convention. Therefore, Slocum "get[s] laid" on all his business trips because he "feel[s] the country, the company, and society expect [him] to" (435; ch. 6). Of course, social pressure is Slocum's excuse, rather than his reason, for modeling his sexual operations on corporate operations. His desire to "fuck" women (with all the power play and sadistic mastery this phrase connotes) is psychologically in harmony with the company's practice of metaphorically "fucking" everyone it can, because Slocum wants the sense of power and emotional insulation such an attitude provides. Thus, as he puts it, he likes to "preserve the distinction between executive and subordinate, employer and employee, even in bed. (*Especially* in bed.)" (42; ch. 2). It is not surprising, therefore, that this character often experiences sexual encounters as if he were watching them through the eyes of a third person:

> I remember the first time I committed adultery. (It wasn't much good.)
> "Now I am committing adultery," I thought.
> It was not much different from the first time I laid my wife after we were married:
> "Now I am laying my wife," I thought. (508; ch. 6)

Here Heller points to a phenomenology of commodification that can help us expand upon Baudrillard's notion that the pleasure of sign-exchange value is pleasure in abstraction. The mechanical tone of this passage bespeaks the sexlessness and joylessness of the act as Slocum often experiences it. Even when the sign-exchange value of a sexual encounter provides an enjoyable experience, as when he takes his wife to a luxurious hotel, it is a narcissistic pleasure enjoyed in isolation. Like

Trina lying naked among the gold coins covering her bed in Frank Norris's *McTeague* (277; ch. 19), Slocum's sexual encounters with his wife in expensive hotels enact the symbolic identification of sex with money and illustrate the masturbatory insulation provided by sign-exchange value. Like masturbation, pleasure as an abstraction, because it insulates one from emotional contact with the other, is pleasure that is safe. Thus, when Slocum commodifies his sex partners, including his wife, he uses the relationship to deny relatedness.

Despite the striking resemblance between Slocum's behavior and corporate operations, his long-awaited promotion to the head of the Sales Department does not bring with it the perfect, placid corporate inwardness he expected. Slocum's thoughts after his promotion consist of his usual litany of worries and self-doubts:

> When I am fifty-five, I will have nothing more to look forward to than Arthur Baron's job and reaching sixty-five. When I am sixty-five, I will have nothing more to look forward to than reaching seventy-five, or dying before then. And when I am seventy-five, I will have nothing more to look forward to than dying before eighty-five, or geriatric care in a nursing home. I will have to take enemas. (Will I have to be dressed in double-layer, waterproof undershorts designed especially for incontinent gentlemen?) I will be incontinent. (561; ch. 8)

Significantly, it is only with the death of his older son that Slocum finally acquires the placid, passive corporate inwardness he seeks.

In many ways, Slocum's "boy," as he calls him (we never learn his name), can be seen as an uncommodified version of himself. Father and son share the same fears and sensibilities, and Slocum usually intermingles thoughts about his son with thoughts about himself: "When I think of him, I think of me" (160; ch. 4). In fact, his boy's troubles are largely a projection of his own: "He won't take chances he doesn't have to. (Neither will I. . . .) He has never, to my knowledge, been in a fist fight. (I wouldn't get in one now either unless it was clearly a matter of life or death. The apple has not fallen far from the tree.)" (289; ch. 4). However, while Slocum, like his wife and daughter, has commodified himself and his world, this nine-year-old child has not. Slocum's boy freely gives away cookies, candy, and money to other children and lets them play with his brand-new toys. And he does so simply for the joy of giving:

"I was happy" [he tells his father]. . . .
"And whenever I feel happy . . . I like to give something away. . . . "
"Why were you happy?"
"Now it gets a little crazy."
"Go ahead. You're not crazy."
"Because I knew I was going to give it away."
(302; ch. 5)

Slocum is "charmed extremely by his [child's] peculiar generosity . . . and beguiling good nature" (286; ch. 5). Yet he tries to change his son without even understanding why: "Why did we proscribe and threaten and interrogate? (Why did we feel so affronted?)" (286; ch. 5). The protagonist knows that his official reason for trying to make the boy more selfish—to teach him to respect the value of money—is a lie: the child understands money very well, and the sums involved are always less than a dime. The real reason for Slocum's difficulty with his son's generosity is that the boy is a projection of his own ego—which may be why he never refers to his son by name—and he feels personally taken advantage of by his son's friends: "I never could stand to see him taken advantage of. It was as though I myself were undergoing the helpless humiliation of being tricked, turned into a sucker. My own pride and ego would drip with wounded recognition" (284; ch. 5).

This kind of projection is also why the boy's presence in the family is so disruptive for Slocum. His son is like a vulnerable part of himself that he can't entirely control; therefore, as long as the boy lives, the father will be subjected to feelings beyond his control. And as long as there remains this uncommodified part of himself, Slocum cannot achieve the escape from existential inwardness he seeks. The only solution is his son's death, a solution that is accomplished by Slocum himself: when the child is superficially wounded in a traffic accident, he hugs him to his breast and smothers him.

Although Slocum is panic-stricken and acts without premeditation when he kills his son, the boy's death is not the kind of genuine accident many critics claim it is: Slocum does not accidentally destroy "what he most wants to save" (LeClair 80).[3] While the protagonist does not plan the act, his commission of it is a function of his desire for his son's death. Slocum's obsessive fear throughout the novel that his son will be killed, and his inability to picture the boy beyond the age of nine, reveal that he wishes, if only unconsciously, for the boy's death. Heller plays with this idea throughout the novel, as when Slocum tells us, "Poor

Oedipus has been much maligned. He didn't want to kill his father. His father wanted to kill *him*" (336; ch. 5), or when he muses about his disappointment in his son's inability to adjust to life's difficulties as other children do: "Maybe I am disappointed in him. . . . Maybe that's why he's scared I want to take him somewhere strange and dangerous and leave him there. Maybe I do" (341; ch. 5). Slocum's desire for his son's death is especially significant just before the scene in which the boy dies. Referring to his son's recent independent behavior he says, "I want my little boy back. . . . I don't want to lose him. I do" (561; ch. 8). The reader is thus cued, right before this pivotal scene, to consider the protagonist's desire to be rid of the boy. His first words after he learns that he has smothered the boy contribute to the feeling that there is something deliberate about the act because they reveal the self-protective mode in which he is operating throughout the incident: "Don't tell my wife" (562; ch. 8). His request is honored: no one but the medical personnel involved ever finds out that Slocum is responsible for his son's death.

In a sense, the killing of the son is a suicide on the part of the father: he kills the part of himself that refused to be co-opted and commodified. However, Slocum's act by no means includes the positive achievement implied by Stephen W. Potts's statement that "Slocum has smothered with his son the phobias that were unbalancing his mind" (44). In fact, all the seemingly positive changes noted in the protagonist as a result of his son's death—for example, Sorkin's suggestion that Slocum is thereby "released from tensions and obligations" (48) and Carton's observation that the boy's death grants Slocum greater authority, both in his life and in his narration of the novel (44)—are a function of the protagonist's escape from existential inwardness, an escape that engenders an almost sociopathic lack of feeling for others.

Freed from the burden of emotion, Slocum becomes the perfect corporate image, inside as well as outside: he is calm, in control, and very, very cold-blooded—an excellent corporate strategist in all phases of his life. In order to remedy his home life, he tells his wife that he loves her, buys her a new house and car, and sends her shopping for furniture; he also buys his daughter the car she'd been lobbying for. And he decides to postpone institutionalizing Derek for a few more years and keep him at home instead. He takes things in hand at work by firing or retiring the "dead wood" and by forcing his sales staff to perform the useless paperwork they'd managed to avoid under their former boss.

These changes do not represent the "self-healing" to which Potts refers (44), but the successful repression of the protagonist's emotional vulnerability. He can finally tell his wife he loves her because he is no longer emotionally vulnerable to her; because the admission no longer has any meaning for him, he relinquishes no power in making it. He can get the behavior he wants from his wife and daughter simply by buying it. He no longer feels the need to send Derek away because he is no longer disturbed by the child's condition. And he can eliminate the people at work he used to feel sorry for—or force them into jobs they don't want—because their plight no longer touches him.[4]

This transformation is underscored by the abrupt change in the language of the narrative in the brief final chapter immediately following the boy's death. This chapter shows us the new Bob Slocum at the office. His monologue now focuses on how well he's doing: his thoughts are about his successful adjustment to his new job and the control he has taken of things at work and at home. There is no more tortured consciousness, no more fears or worries. The novel ends with this brief chapter because the protagonist has no more inwardness to recount; he has put an end to self-reflection, which is the stuff of which the novel is composed. However, that his emotions are successfully repressed by, rather than replaced by, the signifying system is shown by his fleeting "I miss my boy" (568; ch. 9), sandwiched between a description of his improving golf game and Martha the typist's nervous breakdown. Although Slocum can't keep this one emotion from emerging, he is able to quickly shuffle it out of sight beneath his accumulation of career-related concerns.

The point here is that the corporate signifying system is able to insulate him emotionally only when aided by a desire for insulation so strong that it leads him to eliminate the son who has kept him grounded in existential contingency. The parenthetical observations that have continually erupted throughout the narrative no longer consist of flashbacks to his lost youth and flash-forwards to his fears about the future. As we can see in the following passage, parentheses that used to be filled with the overflow of repressed emotions are now filled with the empty sound of moving air from his golf swing:

> I meet a much higher class of executive at Arthur Baron's now when he has us to dinner. I play golf with a much better class of people. (Swish.) I have played golf at Round Hill twice already as a guest of Horace White, once with his undistinguished sister and her husband. She made eyes at

me. (Swish.) I have a hitch in my swing. I have played at Burning Tree in Washington as the guest of a buyer and heard a deputy cabinet official tell an old joke poorly. I laughed. (Swish.) I laughed rambunctiously. (568; ch. 9)

And these parenthetical "swishes" are celebratory, triggered by Slocum's realization that he has acquired the place he has longed for in the corporate structure, the place where celebration is fundamentally empty (swish) because emptiness is what is being celebrated.

Perhaps the protagonist's new ability to handle emotionally charged situations with no emotional engagement is best illustrated by his handling of the office typist's nervous breakdown, the event that closes the novel. Martha's problem had been obvious for months, and Slocum had lived in fear of her breaking down at work—what would he do? Now, however, he says,

I took charge like a ballet master.
"Call Medical," I directed with an authority that was almost musical. "Call personnel. Get Security. Call Travel and tell them to hire a chauffeured limousine immediately."
Martha sits in her typist's chair like an obdurate statue and will not move or speak. She is deaf to entreaty, shakes helping hands off violently, gives signs she might shriek. I wait nearby with an expression of aplomb. . . .
We have a good-sized audience now, and I am the supervisor. Martha rises compliantly, smiling, with a hint of diabolical satisfaction, I see, at the wary attention she has succeeded in extorting from so many people who are solicitous and alarmed. . . .
"Be gentle with her," I adjure. "She's a wonderful girl."
I hear applause when she's gone for the way I handled it.
No one was embarrassed.
Everyone seems pleased with the way I've taken command. (568–69; ch. 9)

Slocum's tone in this passage, as in the passage just before, bespeaks a consciousness that consists of complacency—complacency in his lack of feelings, in the fact that he can finally number himself among the upper-echelon executives who "seem dead" (13; ch. 2).

As we have seen, an awareness of the contingency of life and death is, for Sartre, the source of the possibility of existential growth, an occasion for the assumption of personal responsibility for one's being and actions. Denial of personal responsibility, refusal to undertake the existential project, is, Sartre maintains, the product of bad faith, a kind of self-delusion in which one places the responsibility for one's behavior outside oneself (*Being and Nothingness* 47–70). The notion of bad faith thus resonates with the Socratic equation of evil with ignorance. Sartre does not account for the possibility that one can, without self-delusion as a crutch, refuse the existential project, that one can, knowingly and without the denial of personal responsibility, opt for death-in-life.

Most readers of *Something Happened* don't account for this possibility either. John W. Aldridge (40), Kurt Vonnegut, Jr. (95), and Joseph Epstein (100) don't believe that the protagonist makes any choice at the novel's end; for them, Slocum remains essentially unchanged. Potts sees an important change in Slocum in the final chapter, but he perceives it as a necessary—and therefore healthy—adjustment to a Kafkaesque world (44). For Robert Merrill (91-93, 96), Nicholas Canady (106), and Adam Sorkin (51), the novel's ending portrays a corporate victory in which the protagonist gives up some positive value toward which he was striving.[5] Although Susan Strehle recognizes that the protagonist's problems cannot simply be laid at the feet of a deterministic social order, her claim that *Something Happened* is an existential critique of Slocum's bad faith (107–8) ignores the novel's resistance to the Sartrean framework she employs. Almost every instance of Slocum's self-delusion is shattered by a self-reflection, often sardonic, that cuts through the pleasant illusion and shows Slocum to himself, and to us, in no uncertain terms, as we can see in the following passage in which he indulges in a moment of nostalgic fantasy about Virginia:

> What a deal I blew. . . . What good tits I could have been nibbling on all those months, instead of those . . . sandwiches my mother made for me to take to the city for lunch to save money. . . . I'd lick her lips and large breasts now with my salmon-and-tomato tongue. No, I wouldn't; everything would be the same; if I had her now and I was the one who was older, I would probably be calculating my ass off trying to keep free of her. . . . (362; ch. 6)

As Merrill puts it, "No one is more critical of his behavior, or more perceptive about it, than Slocum himself" (89).

Thus, although the novel begins with the protagonist's fundamental anxiety about being, which is, according to the existential view, the precursor of either existential engagement or bad faith, Slocum follows neither route. As we have seen, he does not undertake the existential project: he does not become the author of his own authentic existence who makes decisions based on a responsible engagement with a life maximized by the knowledge that it is temporally limited. And of utmost importance in terms of an existentialist reading, neither does he delude himself about his responsibility for the avoidance of such a project. Without the bad faith that would tie the novel to an existential understanding of subjectivity, Slocum chooses the path of nonengagement, of death-in-life. Thus, while he does change at the novel's close, his change reveals neither a defeat before the overpowering corporation nor a necessary adjustment to a stultifying corporate reality. Slocum's change in the final chapter reveals a choice, the achievement of a conscious goal. We may find the choice bankrupt, but to say that it is the result of bad faith is to seek a guarantee the novel does not offer.

If, as Walter Davis suggests, subjectivity corresponds to its historical moment (*Inwardness and Existence* 44–45), then *Something Happened* indicates that history has outstripped *Being and Nothingness*, for Slocum's interiority is beyond the existential problematic that informs such works as *The House of Mirth, The Great Gatsby, Death of a Salesman*, and *The Crying of Lot 49*. While Lily Bart, Jay Gatsby, and Willy Loman attempt to escape existential inwardness, the bad faith they inevitably rely upon to help them, and their failure, finally, to succeed, keep them within the existential problematic. And as we have seen, while the difficulties of Oedipa Maas's quest for an existential subjectivity put that subjectivity on trial, the very fact of her quest grounds the text in the existential problematic. Heller's protagonist, however, achieves an inwardness that insulates both himself and the text from the existential problematic, an inwardness that puts him just where Jean Baudrillard places the postmodern subject: "at the controls of a hypothetical machine, isolated in a position of perfect and remote sovereignty, at an infinite distance from his universe of origin" ("Ecstasy" 128). It may be impossible, finally, to eliminate emotion, but Slocum succeeds in eliminating reflection. He has, if I may be permitted the metaphor, put his internal radio dial between stations and replaced the sound of voices with static; the voices may still be there, but he has found a way not to hear them. Thus, while *The Crying of Lot 49* reveals the emptiness of the postmodern cultural landscape, *Something Happened* reveals the emptiness of the postmodern psyche.

If a nondialectical, or linear, notion of causality were ever useful in explaining human behavior, *Something Happened* suggests that it cannot be used to understand the postmodern psyche. For in this novel there is not, as many critics imply, some pristine subjectivity prior to the corporation and then contaminated by it. Rather, the individual and the corporation are responsible for each other: Slocum serves the corporation's desire for socioeconomic hegemony; the corporation serves his desire to escape existential inwardness. And as we have seen, both projects are grounded in an insular depersonalization of self and other that signals the condition of the larger culture in which they are contained: the culture of the American dream. If *The Crying of Lot 49* asks whether or not existential subjectivity can still constitute itself once the individual and the socius are dissolved in a symbiotic system of self-emptying signs, then *Something Happened* does not offer an optimistic response. For Heller's novel suggests that our capacity to constitute an existential subjectivity becomes a moot point when our deepest desire is to escape it.

Conclusion

Commodity Psychology in
American Literature and Culture

The preceding chapters constitute an Althusserian analysis of the American dream as commodity, using a dialectical model of existential subjectivity both to expand Althusser's concept of the relationship between psychology and ideology, and to reformulate the traditional Americanist notion of the relationship between the individual and the socius. Certainly, I do not wish to argue that commodity psychology is the only manifestation or the "first cause" of our psychological politics—or the only mirror in which it is reflected in the literary works examined. There are many factors involved in the production and expression—including artistic expression—of any cultural phenomenon. And any attempt to isolate a first cause for human behavior, in a literary work or in the world, is, surely, a dubious project. The notion of causality as it applies to the humanities and the social sciences is, I think, best understood as multiple, circular, and evolving, rather than as conforming to some hierarchical or linear order. What I do claim for this study is (1) that I've demonstrated Americanists' need for a model of subjectivity to take us, as Davis's model does, beyond the social-individual dichotomy in which American literary criticism tends to stall; and (2) that such a model has allowed me to illuminate the ways in which commodity psychology informs the overall design of our cultural fabric, as the works of Wharton, Fitzgerald, Miller, Pynchon, and Heller illustrate.

As we have seen, the protagonists in *The House of Mirth*, *The Great Gatsby*, *Death of a Salesman*, and *Something Happened*, and the minor characters in *The Crying of Lot 49*, are all driven by the desire to escape existential inwardness. In each text, this transcendental project informs consciousness and structures behavior. Gatsby's obsessive pursuit of

Daisy is the result of his desire to cancel his personal history and escape the existential interiority that history presses upon him: if he can possess Daisy—who, for him, embodies the emotional insulation afforded by the world of upper-class wealth—then he will be transformed into the Jay Gatsby he has heretofore only impersonated, the Jay Gatsby whose family really is of traditional, upper-class stock, the Jay Gatsby who really did travel throughout Europe like a "young rajah" (66) and graduate from Oxford, the Jay Gatsby who is immune to historical contingency. Similarly, if Lily Bart can attain a permanent position in the beau monde of the Trenor-Dorset clique (her project in the first part of the novel) or reify herself as Selden's ideal partner in the "republic of the spirit" (her project in the novel's final chapters), then, she believes, she will be beyond the existential inwardness produced by the demands and contingencies of the physical and emotional universe in which she is vulnerable to other human beings. Even Willy Loman—whose material desires seem so small, and reasonable, next to those of a Jay Gatsby or a Lily Bart—shares with these characters the desire to escape existential inwardness: the complex pattern of avoidance and denial that informs the five regressive episodes structuring the play is grounded in Willy's desire to become the image of socioeconomic success he has worshiped his whole life and thereby to escape his awareness of his failure as a salesman and a father.

It is no surprise, really, that Fitzgerald, Wharton, and Miller have their protagonists die at the end of their narratives: given the failure of the transcendental project in each case, there is no other place for them to go—death is the only transcendence left them. Analogously, the minor characters in *The Crying of Lot 49* either lose their minds entirely in order to lose existential inwardness, as in Mucho's case, or spin their wheels in various kinds of obsessive behavior aimed, albeit unsuccessfully, at getting their transcendental projects off the ground. And although Oedipa's existential engagement, and inwardness, only increase over the course of the novel, the whole point of her experience is to put into question whether or not a genuine existential subjectivity can be constituted in a culture devoted to escaping it. While Heller's Bob Slocum is, in one sense, an exception to this pattern—he succeeds where the others fail, both socioeconomically and in his escape from existential inwardness—the very nature of his success shows that he shares the project, and the desire, of the other characters. In fact,

Slocum's achievement illustrates most explicitly what the other works imply: that the desire to escape historical contingency and the desire to die are both grounded in the desire to escape existential inwardness. For it is clear that Slocum's goal in escaping existential interiority is to achieve accidie, or death-in-life.

How does commodity psychology serve this transcendental project? As *The Great Gatsby* makes especially clear, commodity psychology facilitates the escape from existential inwardness primarily through displacement and mystification. When one desires the kind of control— over life, over contingency, over interiority—that can't be acquired historically, in the real world, one can use the commodity, especially in its sign-exchange value, as a domain in which one can believe such control is possible. And the American dream, because it ties the spiritual domain to the commodity, is the expression of this belief. Thus, one of the central paradoxes of the American dream is that, while it claims to open history to everyone, to allow each individual the opportunity to become a part of American history, in reality it closes off history: it allows each individual the opportunity to escape from history into the commodity. The commodity, then—whether in the form of an object or a person— becomes the site of displacement, the sign that one needs to acquire if one is to feel in control, protected, safe. That is, the commodity becomes, like a religious relic, the site of mystification, of magical thinking. Thus, the commodity is endowed, not just with social meaning, as Marx suggests, but with metaphysical meaning as well. Like the lighting of votive candles or the saying of the rosary, like the repetition of a special mantra or the acquisition of a relic with special indulgences attached to it, the purchase of the right commodities can make good things happen. That is, the commodity can provide an escape from existential interiority that can make it *seem* as if good things are happening.

Of course, commodity psychology in American culture is not confined to the twentieth century. However, it seems to have become ubiquitous in our society with the passage of time. For two factors in twentieth-century American culture have conspired to promote commodity psychology: the decline of religion and the increasing media promotion of readily available consumer goods. Once religion ceased to be a central factor in American life, we needed another source of those psychological balms religion had supplied: the promise of a better life to come, a purpose to orient the direction of our lives from day to day, a source of distraction from the painfulness of life in the here and now, and, as I have explained, a site for magical thinking and the "guarantees" it brings with it. Commodity psychology may not provide happiness, but, like religion, it can distract us from our unhappiness. Perhaps this is why, as my selected texts illustrate, the American dream has sold so well across gender, class, and time period, and why commodity psychology has become such a common phenomenon in our culture.

Indeed, the power of the desire to escape the here and now is illustrated in the protagonists' nostalgia for some lost past in which they seem to remember a better life. Lily recalls her carefree days before her father's financial ruin; Gatsby longs to return to the time when he first courted Daisy; Willy is obsessed with the days when his sons were young; Oedipa thinks nostalgically about the stable, unified identity she used to have at Kinneret-Among-the-Pines; and Slocum yearns to return to his early childhood, before, he believes, "something must have happened" to give him the tortured psyche he suffers from through most of the novel.

Yet these literary works suggest that, in reality, there was no time of perfect wholeness in these characters' pasts. Could Lily Bart return to her young womanhood, she would still have to face her dilemma over marriage: given her mother's spending, her father's money would never have come close to what a Percy Gryce could offer her, and Mrs. Bart would have insisted her daughter marry a fortune far greater than her father's. Similarly, the success of Gatsby's initial courtship of Daisy was based on his false identity, and he would have lost her once the war was over whether or not she had married someone else in his absence. The happy young family Willy Loman believes he once had never really existed: they were barely making ends meet, and his young sons were selfish and brutal, much like their father. The stable, unified identity Oedipa seems to think she had as a suburban "young married" was actually a zombie state rather than an identity. And Bob Slocum's youth wasn't any different from his adulthood: he has felt inadequate and frightened all his life. Thus, it seems that our longing for a "golden past" doesn't mean that such a past ever existed. Rather, it is an indication of our discomfort with the present and with the uncertainty of the future. One must wonder if even the pre-Oedipal longing that seems to play such a ubiquitous role in psychoanalytic theory—drive theorists and object-relations theorists, both of whom posit the existence of an earlier state for which we long, argue merely over whether or not that state is objectless—isn't just symptomatic of a similar desire. Clearly, if commodity psychology can provide even an illusory balm for such pain, it is no wonder that it sells so well.

Obviously, this explanation of why the role of the commodity in American life has become more important and pervasive over time is based on cultural observation and theoretical speculation rather than on the literary texts examined. Nevertheless, there is a kind of chronological "trajectory," which can be traced from the Wharton text through the Heller, suggesting that the nature of the commodity's role has changed over time in a way that might lend support to my speculations. To begin with, *The House of Mirth* (1905), *The Great Gatsby* (1925), *Death of a Salesman* (1949), *The Crying of Lot 49* (1966), and *Something Happened* (1974) map paths of change in a number of areas that impinge on any study of twentieth-century cultural psychology. As we have seen, Wharton's, Fitzgerald's, and Miller's protagonists, as well as Pynchon's minor characters, are in collusion with a social system that, in one way or another, oppresses them. However, while the main characters in the first four works have needs and feelings that conflict with the demands of the milieus to which they aspire or, in the case of Oedipa Maas, in which she finds herself adrift, Bob Slocum is able to deliberately and consciously restructure his consciousness—to repress conflicting needs and feelings—to fit the utterly commodified operational template of the corporation for which he works. And the conscious deliberateness with which Slocum achieves his psychological merger with the corporation is a factor that, in some ways, evolves progressively from Wharton's text to Heller's.

Of the five protagonists, Lily Bart is the only one who at least sustains the attempt to imagine an alternative to her commodified world. Her project, in the closing chapters of the novel, to reify herself as Selden's ideal partner in his "republic of the spirit"—while grounded, like her earlier project to reify herself as an expensive objet d'art, in her desire to escape existential inwardness—is nevertheless different in that it occurs outside the domain of exchange and sign-exchange value. She can remain in the commodified Trenor-Dorset milieu as long as she does only by acting in bad faith, for she cannot permit herself to live their life-style fully conscious of what she is doing.

In contrast, for Jay Gatsby, nothing occurs outside the realm of the commodity, and consciousness, for him, is purely a matter of magical thinking: he believes that the commodity will buy him Daisy and that possession of Daisy will buy him a new personal history and a new identity. Perhaps in order for Gatsby to grapple with the Hegelian unhappy consciousness that the other characters are forced to deal with—and perhaps for Fitzgerald to be able to imagine Gatsby's consciousness in this way at all—this character would have to survive the loss of Daisy, and the failure of his transcendental project, by more than just a few hours.

Unlike Gatsby, Willy Loman knows, on some level, that his commodified goals are empty. This is the knowledge he spends the play trying his best to repress—to the point of suicide when ordinary methods of avoidance and denial no longer suffice. He can't give up his idea that the American dream must be a realm of absolute positive values. Certainly, Willy Loman would like to acquire whatever consciousness would permit him the kind of success Bob Slocum has. However, given the ideological tools available in Willy's time and place, he wouldn't be able to imagine how a consciousness like Slocum's—aware of its own poverty—could ever be rewarded in a world structured by the American dream, which, Willy believes, demands a certain kind of "positive" consciousness. And while Oedipa Maas is horrified by the utterly commodified, existentially impoverished terrain that is postmodern America, she can only wait for something to change, for she is paralyzed by her inability to sustain any projection of a world beyond the one she sees.

Finally, Bob Slocum is very conscious of exactly how corrupt and meaningless his goals are—he's very articulate about that—but he also knows he wants to achieve them anyway. And he is willing and able to do whatever it takes to succeed. Thus, from Lily Bart to Bob Slocum we see a progressively deeper and more self-conscious psychological investment in a world stuctured by the commodity.

We also see a progressive emptying of the sign. I have argued that all five works reveal the structures of psychological investments in sign-exchange value, which, by definition, is not based upon the object qua object, for the object's material existence is, strictly speaking, a function of use value only. The sign can nevertheless be inhabited by the object, I think, to the extent that the sign associates social meaning with some physical experience of the object. For example, for Lily Bart, *part* of her desire for a permanent position among the Trenor-Dorset clique is based upon her capacity to enjoy the physical comforts of luxurious surroundings. As I observed in my analysis of Wharton's protagonist, a beautiful environment is not, as most critics would have it, the ultimate reason for Lily's single-minded dedication to the Trenor-Dorset milieu. Were that the case, she would have been equally happy with the Sam Gormers. However, for Lily, the sign of social status is associated with the enjoyment of luxurious comfort, and her capacity to appreciate such comfort is very well developed. For Lily, sign-exchange value does not obliterate use value; indeed, sign-exchange value often evokes use value, and vice versa.

For Jay Gatsby, the sign is not so full. His mansion, his car, and his hydroplane have little significance to him beyond their function as signs of his arrival at a social level that will allow him to pursue Daisy—another sign—with a success he was unable to achieve the first time around. Willy Loman's relationship to the sign is even somewhat more removed from the sign's content. While Jay Gatsby succeeds in acquiring most of the signs he desires and picks the correct signs for his purposes, Willy Loman fails to acquire the signs he wants, and the signs he wants do not have the content he thinks they have. He never acquires the image, the persona, of the well-liked man, and even if he did learn to behave with the panache he thinks is its sign, such a personality would not necessarily be related to business or parental success.

The postmodern terrain in which Oedipa Maas has lost her way empties the sign even further: it is a terrain dominated by simulation, empty commodity signs that offer nonthreatening, fetishized abstractions in place of authentic experience. However, while Oedipa's consciousness—her desire to decipher this profusion of apparently undecipherable signs, and the existential engagement that such a desire implies—at least maintains the desire for and possibility of meaningful signification, Bob Slocum's utterly abstract relationship to his own experience by the end of *Something Happened* empties the sign of all possibility. In the flat consciousness Slocum exhibits in the novel's closing pages, all thoughts coexist on a single affective plane, an affective plane marked, ironically, by its lack of affect. His narrative, like the signs of corporate success that constitute it, suggests only surfaces. All signs are now corporate signs: they point to concepts such as profit, loss, and power, with no reference to what it is that has been gained or lost, empowered or disempowered. That is, signs have become mathematical functions: it's the x, y, and z that count, rather than the nature of the quantity that occupies a given position in the formula.

In many ways, contemporary Americans face the same problem faced by Lily Bart, Jay Gatsby, Willy Loman, Oedipa Maas, and Bob Slocum—and by their authors: how to imagine a world, and constitute a consciousness, outside the psychosocial framework structured by the commodity. Indeed, the commodification of American culture today is as thorough, if not always quite as obvious, as the industrial transformation of American culture was in the nineteenth century. As we have seen, commodity psychology is operating whenever we are invited—or invite ourselves—to replace the problematics of interiority with the semiotics of prestige, whenever we fetishize the signifier, or the sign system itself, and thereby acquire, however transiently, some measure of emotional insulation against existential contingency.

Fetishization of the signifier is the primary operation, of course, in America's obsession with fashion in any form, including trends in apparel, motor vehicles, architecture, food, the arts, interior decorating, and even psychological self-help techniques (which, themselves, often consist of methods for avoiding existential inwardness so that we can "feel good about ourselves" whether we should feel good or not). As this short but representative list illustrates, commodity psychology collapses the profound dimensions of human experience with the mundane by transforming them both into abstractions, into functions of the signifier. Indeed, the purpose of commodity psychology is to trivialize the profound in order to render it less emotionally threatening.

Of course, commodity psychology is also evident in America's obsession with the act of purchasing itself, illustrated in the popular "shop 'til you drop" slogan—which, although originally intended to spoof obsessive shopping, became its proud "call to arms"—and in the accumulation of money or goods beyond any reasonable uses to which they might be put. Perhaps the most obvious, and the most humorous, examples of commodity psychology can be found in specific consumer products, such as the Cellular Phoney, a fake car telephone produced by Faux Systems, an American company whose corporate slogan is "It's not what you own; it's what people think you own."

In a subtler fashion, the fetishization of the signifier is also the operative element in America's fascination with simulacra: for example, amusement facilities, such as those promoted by the Disney Corporation, in which exotic geographic locations and historical figures and events are presented in simulated form unnervingly reminiscent of *Lot 49*'s Fangoso Lagoons. Indeed, Jean Baudrillard's *America* is largely an examination of the success of simulacra in the United States or, perhaps more precisely, an examination of the ways in which American culture today *is* simulacra, constituted by the obsession with abstraction, because that which exists in the abstract is, by virtue of its separation from the world of existential contingency, emotionally nonthreatening.

Those of us in academia are perhaps most familiar with the fetishization of the signifier in terms of the runaway careerism evident in the hegemony of the professional image. Here, commodity psychology is evident in the quantification of publication as the determining factor in hiring, promotion, and salary decisions; the "star system" by which prestigious universities compete with one another in terms of the name recognition of their faculty, rather than the quality of education offered their students; and, at the lower rungs of the university ladder, the selection of dissertation topics solely for their perceived marketability and the growing problem, for hiring committees, of "paper candidates" who barely resemble, during the job interview let alone in the classroom, the academic image created by their résumés.

The most frightening examples of commodity psychology can probably be found in the media's commodification of the news, which is, for all intents and purposes, the commodification of history. The most striking example of this phenomenon is the media's commodification of the Gulf War—"Operation Desert Storm"—which was portrayed for television viewers, as some commentators noted, as if it were the Superbowl instead of a military operation. It wasn't simply a case of "selling" the war to the American people; all military actions must be "sold" to the public, which is why, for example, the nuclear annihilation of Hiroshima and Nagasaki in 1945 was sold to historians as a "necessary evil." The issue here is that the Gulf War was sold as a surface without an interior—as a sporting event in which the home team was pitted against an opponent it could "clobber" before the end of the first quarter without even sending out the first string—and, as such, its appeal lay in the escape from existential inwardness it offered within a context having the potential to engage that inwardness to its maximum capacity.

Of course, not all manifestations of commodity psychology are readily visible. However, if we remember that the commodity is not the source of desire but the site upon which desire is displaced—a cultural surface upon which we can project and deny disturbing aspects of our own interiority—we can begin to observe the relationship between the fetishization of the signifier and heretofore apparently unrelated phenomena. The most radical example of the kind of cultural psychology to which such projection points is violent crime, which I touch upon here merely as an example of the range of psychosocial phenomena commodity psychology can help us begin to understand. To return to the theoretical "laboratory" provided by literature, Bret Easton Ellis's *American Psycho* provides us with a useful, and horrifying, example.

Like *The Great Gatsby*, *American Psycho* puts subject (interior) and object (exterior) on a par—and the object dominates. Protagonist Patrick Bateman is obsessed with his physical appearance, his image, and with the ownership of specific, brand-name consumer products that created and sustain his image. Like *Death of a Salesman* and *Something Happened*, Ellis's novel shows us that the flip side of psychological projection is internalization: Loman, Slocum, and Bateman simultaneously project onto the cultural surface the inwardness they want to avoid and, in its place, internalize that same cultural surface. In other words, they use the commodity—the fetishization of the signifier, the cultural surface—to "launder" their interiority. Both Slocum, at the novel's close, and Bateman, from the opening pages, illustrate inwardness with no otherness, no separateness from its social milieu: each is an interior wholly constituted by the cultural exterior. However, while Slocum, after the death of his son, represents the placid, anesthetized manifestation of this psychology, Bateman represents its criminal possibility: the psychological imperative to destroy all perceived threats against his maintenance of the emotional insulation that *is* his identity, within an environment filled with such threats.

This last example illustrates, in very speculative terms, what I hope the preceding chapters have revealed much more concretely: that the implications of commodity psychology, and of the merger of ideology and psychology in general, are legion. That these implications have remained, for the most part, unexplored by American literary criticism reveals, I think, both the absence of critical tools with which to perceive such phenomena and the importance of recognizing those tools when they are set before us. An existential understanding of the dialectics of psyche and socius—of our psychological politics—offers us those tools. With them, we can open American literature and the culture it represents to a new domain for American literary criticism strikingly relevant to the current theoretical impasse in conceptualizing subjectivity and the social crisis it reflects. Without a thoroughly existentialized dialectical model of subjectivity, our understanding of American literature and culture will remain sorely limited.

Notes

Introduction

1. Critics using this oppositional model as a paradigm for understanding the literature I will be discussing include the following representative sample: Howe, Lyde, Nevius, L. Trilling, Chase, Gallo, Moore, D. Parker, Aarnes, Brucher, Överland, Takács, Quilligan, Costa, and Sorkin.

2. Among the best known of the numerous publications promoting ethical criticism are probably Allan Bloom's *Closing of the American Mind*, Wayne Booth's *Company We Keep*, and Gerald Graff's *Literature Against Itself*.

3. Of course, there have been a number of significant attempts to account for the interaction of the individual and society in terms of the relationship between psychology and ideology, among them Habermas's *Communication and the Evolution of Society*, Jameson's *Political Unconscious*, Luhmann's *Differentiation of Society*, and, earlier, Horkheimer and Adorno's *Dialectic of Enlightenment* and Fromm's *Escape from Freedom*. However, such texts do not provide the kind of dialectical conception of psyche and socius necessary to a full understanding of their existential symbiosis. Such efforts have usually been circumscribed by their reliance upon categories too discrete and static to illuminate the subtle ways in which the terms they separate overlap; or they have been limited by a teleology that inevitably issues in some form of reification reminiscent of Hegel's *Geist*. These forms of reification include a priori, rationalist structures of communication; structuralist semiotics; psychological structures based on the hegemony of the ego; essentialist theories of human nature; and the like.

4. As Williams points out in "Dominant, Residual, and Emergent," history doesn't fit into tidy, chronologically discrete categories. At any given time in the history of a culture, one can isolate what he calls residual, dominant, and emergent values. These are, respectively, values left over from a time past, values that are currently the most pervasive and influential, and values just coming into being.

5. Versions of my chapters on *The House of Mirth*, *Death of a Salesman*, *The Crying of Lot 49*, and *Something Happened* have been published or are forthcoming under the following titles: "Beyond Morality: Lily Bart, Lawrence Selden,

and the Aesthetic Commodity in *The House of Mirth*," *Edith Wharton Review* 9.2 (1992): 3–10; "The Psychological Politics of the American Dream: *Death of a Salesman* and the Case for an Existential Dialectics," *Essays in Literature* 19.2 (1992): 260–78; "Existential Subjectivity on Trial: *The Crying of Lot 49* and the Politics of Despair," *Pynchon Notes*, 28–29 (1991): 5–25; "Joseph Heller's *Something Happened*: The Commodification of Consciousness and the Postmodern Flight from Inwardness," *CEA Critic* 54.2 (1992): 37–51.

Chapter 1

1. For example, Lily Bart has been variously seen as a rather independent, even somewhat rebellious, character (Ammons 30–34, Wershoven 58, Dimock 124), as the victim of an almost naturalistic determinism (Lyde 135, Nevius 56–57), and as her own worst enemy owing either to her tendency to act too quickly (Fryer 90) or to her tendency not to act quickly enough (Auchincloss 24).

2. Other critics who believe that Lily turns to Selden as a moral alternative to the Trenor-Dorset milieu include Dimock (134), Howe (124, 126), Lyde (129), and Walton (66).

3. I do not intend any kind of biological essentialism here. Certainly, men and women both are liable to the same kinds of commodified consciousness and capable of the same kinds of transcendental projects. (Indeed, one task of this chapter will be to explore the symbiotic relationship between Lily's transcendental project and that of Lawrence Selden.) Wharton's novel, however, foregrounds the psychology of self-reification to which women in our culture have, historically, been heir.

4. See, for example, Wershoven, Montgomery (897), Dimock, and Fryer (86).

5. High society then consisted of both old New York families (descendants of British and Dutch colonists) and nouveaux riches (post–Civil War, industrial millionaires) who were marrying/buying their way into the established families. The Gryces, Stepneys, Penistons, and Van Osburghs number among the first group; the Trenors and Dorsets are examples of the second.

6. See, for example, Wolff (116–17), D. Trilling (100), and Howe (124).

7. The belief of some critics that Lily is sexually responsive seems to be based on a confusion of erotic display with erotic feeling or on the fact that the critics themselves find her sexually attractive. See, for example, Fryer (77), McDowell (47), and D. Trilling (113). In contrast, Shulman notes that Lily does not act from "genuine sexual impulses" (16), but he develops the idea differently than I do.

8. See, for example, Wolff (111), Auchincloss (14), Lawson (36), and Walton (60).

9. Shulman discusses the conflict between what he calls Lily's "real self"—her ideal, moral self, which she and Selden associate with timeless

beauty—and her "captive self," the crass, self-serving traits she shares with Bertha Dorset. However, Shulman doesn't interrogate the psychological motives informing the protagonist's desire for the ideal.

10. Nietzsche distinguishes between *morality*, which he defines as adherence to social conventions, and *ethics*, which he defines as the philosophical problematic underlying those conventions. While Wharton's critics use these two terms interchangeably, it is clear from the way in which they use them that the issue here is, in Nietzschean terms, an ethical one: the philosophical implications underlying the adherence to, or breach of, social conventions are the area of critical concern.

11. Although they develop the idea differently than I do, Gimbel (36) and Wolff (116) both compare Lily to a child.

12. There is a good deal of disagreement about the nature and meaning of Lily's death. For a representative sample, see Ammons (37, 42), Fryer (94), McDowell (43–45), and Walton (67). While Lawson believes, as I do, that death is "the only escape left for Lily" (34), he develops the idea differently.

Chapter 2

1. For similar views of Gatsby, see Trilling (234–35, 240–43), Chase (300–301), Gallo (41–43), Parker (34–36, 42–43), Stern (192, 197), and Moore (334). An important exception to this critical consensus is provided by Fussell, who believes that the novel represents Fitzgerald's deliberate and scathing criticism of modern America, of the American dream, and of Jay Gatsby, the representative modern American (46–49).

2. While Harvey observes that Gatsby is Tom's "double," and Lehan notes that Gatsby "grotesquely resembles" Buchanan (111), they develop this idea differently than I do.

3. For example, Allen reduces the character's role in the novel to nothing more than "a symbol for Gatsby" (110), and Burnam finds Daisy unworthy of "any exhaustive analysis" (107).

4. For an interesting argument that Daisy is more cold-bloodedly destructive—and evil—than either Tom or Gatsby, see Lockridge.

5. Three noteworthy exceptions to the tendency to sever Gatsby from his history are Bruccoli (223), Fussell (46–47), and Audhuy (119): they recognize that Gatsby shares the corruption of the world he lives in. However, they develop the implications of this observation differently than I do.

6. At the risk of oversimplification, the power of the commodity to subvert a narrative can be illustrated if one imagines Fassbinder's *Effi Briest* in color. One effect of the film's having been shot in black and white is that the power of the commodity *over the viewer* is thereby reduced: we can see rather clearly how the characters are seduced by their possessions because the black-and-white

screen allows us to remain sufficiently beyond the setting's seductive appeal. It would have been, I think, more difficult to see the role played by setting, by the ubiquitous consumer objects that define so much of the characters' lives, had the setting been rendered à la *Doctor Zhivago* or *The Sound of Music*.

Chapter 3

1. For similar arguments, see, among others, Schlueter and Flanagan, Bigsby, and B. Parker.

2. See, for example, Welland, Brucher, and Innes.

3. Many critics have made this point. See for example, Aarnes, Overland, Steinberg, and Bently. While Williams believes that the psychological and political dramas are fused in the play, he doesn't analyze the nature of this fusion.

4. August notes the importance of Willy's abandonment by his father and suggests that his early lack of a male role model is responsible for many of the male role problems he has as an adult.

5. For a complete discussion of the cultural manifestations of narcissism (including useful comparisons of the work of Freud, Melanie Klein, Heinz Kohut, Otto Kernberg, Christopher Lasch, and others), see Alford.

6. Schneider discusses "the return of the repressed" in the play, but he focuses his analysis on Willy's guilty hatred of Ben and on Biff and Happy's Oedipal murder of their father.

7. See, for example, Bigsby (116), Szondi (21), Mottram (31), and Jackson (16).

8. Of course, Happy's success with the easy "pick-ups" during the restaurant scene is much more believable than his rather outrageous success with the fiancées of his executive coworkers. Although his stories of sexual prowess have the familiar ring of macho exaggeration, there is no sign in the text that we are expected to believe Happy is lying about his sexual exploits with these brides-to-be. This part of Happy's history thus might be an example of how a playwright's fantasy projection can inform characterization.

9. For readers whose familiarity with the play is derived primarily from the Volker Schlöndorff film version (with Dustin Hoffman), it is important to note that the sexual dimension present in Linda's film characterization is not present in the 1949 text of the play. For example, in this film version, in response to Willy's affectionate "Come on, give me a little something," which he says to his wife as he leaves to ask Howard for a New York job, Linda performs a seductive little shimmy and runs gaily into the house. No such interaction between husband and wife occurs in Miller's original version of the play.

10. Hadomi also notes that Willy's suicide is an "act of self-deception"(157). While she doesn't romanticize his suicide, neither does she analyze the motives behind it. She believes that Willy kills himself simply because "in his mind suicide becomes . . . equated with success" (168).

11. Although the set designer, Jo Mielziner, was responsible for the "dreamlike" environment that surrounds the Loman house, Miller liked this aspect of the set, he says, because it "was an emblem of Willy's intense longing for the promises of the past" and "parallel with the script" (*Timebends* 188).

Chapter 4

1. For similar binary readings, see Hunt (40), Takács (302–4), Olsen (161), Quilligan (201), Hays (23, 32), and Green (37). Hite (80, 89), Ward (28–29), and Watson (71) believe, as I do, that while Oedipa's view of her situation rests on a binary understanding of contemporary reality, the text suggests that her view is mistaken; however, they develop this idea differently than I do. In contrast, Palmeri argues that Oedipa "declines the either-or choice that her time presses upon her" (995), and Pearce suggests that Oedipa finally transcends the emotional, if not epistemological, limitations of her binary world through her growing "commit[ment] to human connection" (147).

2. For similar readings of entropy in *Lot 49*, see Takács (297–99), Schaub (51–58), and Tanner (67). In contrast, Mangel might be taken to agree with me that in *Lot 49* thermodynamic entropy and information entropy both tend in the direction of infinite disorder—which I read as utter randomness, nondifferentiation, or sameness—for she does not distinguish the two kinds of entropy at all. Even "the nature of language itself," she observes, "fails [in *Lot 49*] to differentiate and order" (206).

3. For a fairly thorough account of the novel's various levels of uncertainty or indeterminacy, see Olsen.

4. For a complete discussion of the mirror stage, see Lacan's "The Mirror Stage as Formative of the Function of the I."

5. Indeed, Conroy argues, in his superb discussion of American consumer society, that Oedipa's binary logic, itself an American cultural production, supplies throughout the novel the escape she seeks from the painful uncertainties of human connection. Similarly, Dugdale suggests that the protagonist uses the Tristero quest, like a religious quest, to escape the "repugnant aspects of her society" (129). I believe both critics, however, underestimate the degree and sincerity of Oedipa's existential struggle.

Chapter 5

1. Other critics whose readings of the novel rest on the premise that the individual and the socius are interactive but *discrete* entities include, for example, DelFattore, Aldridge, Tucker, LeClair, Vonnegut, Strehle, Canaday, Merrill, and Potts.

2. As Heidegger has observed, fear is the way the inauthentic person lives

his or her anxiety about existential situatedness. For example, the groundless fear that one doesn't have enough life insurance or that one's house will be robbed are externalizations of—and attempts to avoid—this anxiety.

3. See also Merrill (93), Carton (44), Sebouhian (51), and Canaday (104). A noteworthy exception is Strehle, who believes that Slocum "deliberately murders his son" (110).

4. In his discussion of Slocum's "coming of age" in the Lacanian Symbolic order, Mellard acknowledges, but does not analyze, the implications of the protagonist's adjustment to his cultural milieu. Similarly, Sorkin notes, "That Slocum is normal, that in the end he epitomizes his culture, is precisely the problem" (52).

5. In contrast, Tucker notes that Slocum's condition at the novel's close is one he created for himself (328, 340); however, Tucker does not develop the implications of this observation.

Bibliography

Aarnes, William. "Tragic Form and the Possibility of Meaning in *Death of a Salesman.*" *Furman Studies* ns 29 (1983). Rpt. in *Modern Critical Interpretations: Arthur Miller's* Death of a Salesman. Ed. Harold Bloom. New York: Chelsea, 1988. 95–111.

Adams, James Truslow. *The Epic of America.* 1931. Boston: Little, 1955.

Aldridge, John W. *The American Novel and the Way We Live Now.* New York: Oxford UP, 1983.

Alford, C. Fred. *Narcissism: Socrates, the Frankfurt School, and Psychoanalytic Theory.* New Haven: Yale UP, 1988.

Allen, Joan M. *Candles and Carnival Lights: The Catholic Sensibility of F. Scott Fitzgerald.* New York: New York UP, 1978.

Allen, Woody, dir. *Play It Again, Sam.* With Diane Keaton. Paramount, 1972.

Althusser, Louis. "Ideology and Ideological State Apparatuses." 1970. *Lenin and Philosophy and Other Essays.* Trans. Ben Brewster. New York: Monthly Review, 1971. 127–86.

Ammons, Elizabeth. *Edith Wharton's Argument with America.* Athens: U of Georgia P, 1980.

Atkinson, Brooks. Rev. of *Death of a Salesman,* by Arthur Miller. *New York Times* 11 Feb. 1949, sec. 2: 27.

Auchincloss, Louis. *Edith Wharton.* Minneapolis: U of Minnesota P, 1961.

Audhuy, Letha. "The *Waste Land* Myth and Symbols in *The Great Gatsby.*" *Études Anglaises* 33.1 (1980). Rpt. in *Modern Critical Interpretations: F. Scott Fitzgerald's* The Great Gatsby. New York: Chelsea, 1986. 109–22.

August, Eugene R. "*Death of a Salesman*: A Men's Studies Approach." *Western Ohio Journal* (Dayton) 7.1 (1986): 53–71.

Barthes, Roland. *Mythologies.* 1957. Trans. Annette Lavers. New York: Hill, 1979.

Baudrillard, Jean. *America.* 1986. Trans. Chris Turner. New York: Verso, 1988.

——. "The Ecstasy of Communication." Trans. John Johnston. *The Anti-Aesthetic: Essays on Postmodern Culture.* Ed. Hal Foster. Port Townsend, WA: Bay, 1983. 126–34.

——. *For a Critique of the Political Economy of the Sign.* 1972. Trans. Charles Levin. St. Louis: Telos, 1981.

——. *Simulations*. Trans. Paul Foss, Paul Patton, and Philip Beitchman. New York: Semiotext(e), 1983.

Bauer, Dale M. *Feminist Dialogics: A Theory of Failed Community*. Albany: State U of New York P, 1988. 89–127.

Bentley, Eric. "Back to Broadway." *Theatre Arts* 33 (1949): 12, 14.

Bewley, Marius. "Scott Fitzgerald's Criticism of America." *Sewanee Review* 62 (1954): 223–46. Rpt. in *Modern Critical Interpretations: F. Scott Fitzgerald's The Great Gatsby*. Ed. Harold Bloom. New York: Chelsea, 1986. 11–27.

Bigsby, C. W. E. "*Death of a Salesman*: In Memoriam." *A Critical Introduction to Twentieth Century American Drama 2: Tennessee Williams, Arthur Miller, Edward Albee*. Cambridge UP, 1984. 135–248. Rpt. in *Modern Critical Interpretations: Arthur Miller's* Death of a Salesman. Ed. Harold Bloom. New York: Chelsea, 1988. 113–28.

Bloom, Allan. *The Closing of the American Mind*. New York: Simon, 1987.

Bloom, Harold. Introduction. *Modern Critical Interpretations: Arthur Miller's* Death of a Salesman. Ed. Harold Bloom. New York: Chelsea, 1988. 1–5.

Booth, Wayne. *The Company We Keep*. Berkeley: U of California P, 1989.

Bruccoli, Matthew J. *Some Sort of Epic Grandeur: The Life of F. Scott Fitzgerald*. New York: Harcourt, 1981.

Brucher, Richard T. "Willy Loman and *The Soul of a New Machine:* Technology and the Common Man." *Journal of American Studies* 13.3 (1983). Rpt. in *Modern Critical Interpretations: Arthur Miller's* Death of a Salesman. Ed. Harold Bloom. New York: Chelsea, 1988. 83–94.

Burnam, Tom. "The Eyes of Dr. Eckleburg: A Re–Examination of *The Great Gatsby*." *College English* 13 (1952). Rpt. in *F. Scott Fitzgerald: A Collection of Critical Essays*. Ed. Arthur Mizener. Englewood Cliffs: Prentice-Hall, 1963. 104–11.

Camus, Albert. *L'Étranger*. Ed. Germaine Brée. Englewood Cliffs: Prentice-Hall, 1955.

Canady, Nicholas. "Joseph Heller: Something Happened to the American Dream." *CEA Critic* 40.1 (1977): 34–38. Rpt. in *Critical Essays on Joseph Heller*. Ed. James Nagel. Boston: Hall, 1984. 102–6.

Carson, Neil. *Arthur Miller*. New York: Grove, 1982.

Carton, Evan. "The Politics of Selfhood: Bob Slocum, T. W. Garp and Auto-American-Biography." *Novel* 20.1 (1986): 41–61.

Cartwright, Kent. "Nick Carraway as an Unreliable Narrator." *Papers on Language and Literature* 20.2 (1984): 218–32.

Chase, Richard. "*The Great Gatsby*." *The American Novel and Its Traditions*. New York: Doubleday, 1957. 162–67. Rpt. in The Great Gatsby: A Study. Ed. Frederick J. Hoffman. New York: Scribner's, 1962. 297–302.

Conroy, Mark. "The American Way and Its Double in *The Crying of Lot 49*." *Pynchon Notes* 24–25 (1989): 45–70.

Costa, Richard Hauer. "Notes from a Dark Heller: Bob Slocum and the Underground Man." *Texas Studies in Literature and Language* 23.1 (1981): 159–82.

Davis, Walter A. *Get the Guests: Psychoanalysis—Modern American Drama—The Audience.* Madison: U of Wisconsin P, 1994.

——. *Inwardness and Existence: Subjectivity in/and Hegel, Heidegger, Marx, and Freud.* Madison: U of Wisconsin P, 1989.

DelFattore, Joan. "The Dark Stranger in Heller's *Something Happened.*" *Critical Essays on Joseph Heller.* Ed. James Nagel. Boston: Hall, 1984. 127–38.

Di Giuseppe, Rita. "The Shadows of the Gods: Tragedy and Commitment in *Death of a Salesman.*" *Quaderni di lingue e letterature* 14 (1989): 109–28.

Dillon, Andrew. "*The Great Gatsby*: The Vitality of Illusion." *Arizona Quarterly* 44.1 (1988): 49–61.

Dimock, Wai–chee. "Debasing Exchange: Edith Wharton's *The House of Mirth.*" *Edith Wharton.* Ed. Harold Bloom. New York: Chelsea, 1986. 123–37.

Dixon, Roslyn. "Reflecting Vision in *The House of Mirth.*" *Twentieth Century Literature* 33.2 (1987): 211–22.

Dugdale, John. *Thomas Pynchon: Allusive Parables of Power.* New York: St. Martin's, 1990.

Dyson, A. E. "*The Great Gatsby*: Thirty-Six Years After." *Modern Fiction Studies* 7.1 (1961). Rpt.in *F. Scott Fitzgerald: A Collection of Critical Essays.* Ed. Arthur Mizener. Englewood Cliffs: Prentice-Hall, 1963. 112–24.

Eco, Umberto. *Travels in Hyperreality.* 1975. Trans. William Weaver. New York: Harcourt, 1986.

Ellis, Bret Easton. *American Psycho.* New York: Vintage, 1991.

Epstein, Joseph. "Joseph Heller's Milk Train: Nothing More to Express." Rev. of *Something Happened,* by Joseph Heller. *Washington Post Book World* 6 Oct. 1974: 1–3. Rpt. in *Critical Essays on Joseph Heller.* Ed. James Nagel. Boston: Hall, 1984. 97–101.

Fassbinder, Rainer Werner, dir. *Effi Briest.* With Hanna Schygulla. Tango, 1974.

Faulkner, William. *The Wild Palms.* 1939. New York: Vintage, 1966.

Fetterly, Judith. "*The Great Gatsby*: Fitzgerald's *droit de seigneur.*" *The Resisting Reader: A Feminist Approach to American Fiction.* Bloomington: Indiana UP, 1978. 72–100.

Fish, Stanley. "Literature in the Reader: Affective Stylistics." *Reader-Response Criticism.* Ed. Jane P. Tompkins. Baltimore: Johns Hopkins UP, 1980. 70–100.

Fitzgerald, F. Scott. *The Great Gatsby.* 1925. New York: Scribner's, 1953.

——. *The Letters of F. Scott Fitzgerald.* Ed. Andrew Turnbull. New York: Scribner's, 1963.

Flaubert, Gustave. *Madame Bovary.* 1857. Trans. Alan Russell. New York: Penguin, 1950.

Freud, Sigmund. *Beyond the Pleasure Principle.* 1920. *Standard Edition.* Vol. 18. London: Hogarth, 1961. 7–64. 24 vols. 1953– .

——. "The Ego and the Id." 1923. *Standard Edition*. Vol. 19. London: Hogarth, 1962. 12–59. 24 vols. 1953–.

——. "Fetishism." 1927. *Standard Edition*. Vol. 21. London: Hogarth, 1961. 152–57. 24 vols. 1953–.

——. *The Interpretation of Dreams*. 1900. Rpt. in *The Basic Writings of Sigmund Freud*. Trans. Dr. A. A. Brill, ed. New York: Modern Library, 1938. 180–549.

Fromm, Erich. *Escape from Freedom*. New York: Holt, 1961.

Fryer, Judith. *Felicitous Space: The Imaginative Structures of Edith Wharton and Willa Cather*. Chapel Hill: U of North Carolina P, 1986.

Fussell, Edwin. "Fitzgerald's Brave New World." *ELH, Journal of English Literary History* 19 (1952). Rpt. in *F. Scott Fitzgerald: A Collection of Critical Essays*. Ed. Arthur Mizener. Englewoood Cliffs: Prentice-Hall, 1963. 43–56.

Gallo, Rose Adrienne. *F. Scott Fitzgerald*. New York: Ungar, 1978.

Gimbel, Wendy. *Edith Wharton: Orphancy and Survival*. New York: Praeger, 1984.

Giraudoux, Jean. *La guerre de Troie n'aura pas lieu*. Paris: Grasset, 1935.

Goodman, Susan. *Edith Wharton's Women: Friends and Rivals*. Hanover: UP of New England, 1990.

Graff, Gerald. *Literature Against Itself*. Chicago: U of Chicago P, 1979.

Green, Martin. "*The Crying of Lot 49*: Pynchon's Heart of Darkness." *Pynchon Notes* 10 (1982): 30–38.

Habermas, Jürgen. *Communication and the Evolution of Society*. Trans. Thomas McCarthy. New York: Beacon, 1979.

Hadomi, Leah. "Fantasy and Reality: Dramatic Rhythm in *Death of a Salesman*." *Modern Drama* 31 (1988): 157–74.

Hart, Jeffrey. "'Out of it ere night': The WASP Gentleman as Cultural Ideal." *New Criterion* 7.5 (1989): 27–34.

Harvey, W. J. "Theme and Texture in *The Great Gatsby.*" *English Studies* 38 (1957): 12–20. Rpt. in *Twentieth Century Interpretations of* The Great Gatsby. Ed. Ernest Lockridge. Englewood Cliffs: Prentice-Hall, 1968. 90–100.

Haug, Wolfgang Fritz. *Critique of Commodity Aesthetics: Appearance, Sexuality and Advertising in Capitalist Society*. 1971. Trans. Robert Bock. 8th ed. Minneapolis: U of Minnesota P, 1986.

Hayman, Ronald. *Arthur Miller*. London: Heinemann, 1970.

Hays, Peter L. "Pynchon's Cunning Lingual Novel: Communication in *Lot 49*." *University of Mississippi Studies in English* 5 (1984–87): 23–38.

Hegel, G. W. F. "Freedom of Self-consciousness: Stoicism, Scepticism, and the Unhappy Consciousness." *The Phenomenology of Mind*. 1807. Trans. J. B. Baillie. 2nd ed. London: George Allen, 1931. 241–67.

Heidegger, Martin. *Being and Time*. 1927. Trans. John Macquarrie and Edward Robinson. New York: Harper, 1962.

Heller, Joseph. *Something Happened*. New York: Knopf, 1974.

Heyen, William. "Arthur Miller's *Death of a Salesman* and the American

Dream." *American Drama and Theatre in the Twentieth Century*. Ed. Alfred Weber and Siegfried Neuweiler. Göttingen: Vandenhoeck, 1975. Rpt. in *Modern Critical Interpretations: Arthur Miller's* Death of a Salesman. Ed. Harold Bloom. New York: Chelsea, 1988. 47–58.

Hite, Molly. *Ideas of Order in the Novels of Thomas Pynchon*. Columbus: Ohio State UP, 1983.

Horkheimer, Max, and Theodor Adorno. *Dialectic of Enlightenment*. 1944. Trans. John Cumming. New York: Continuum, 1982.

Howe, Irving. "A Reading of *The House of Mirth*." *Edith Wharton: A Collection of Critical Essays*. Ed. Irving Howe. Englewood Cliffs: Prentice-Hall, 1962. 1–18.

Hunt, John W. "Comic Escape and Anti–Vision: *V.* and *The Crying of Lot 49*." Excerpted from "Comic Escape and Anti–Vision: The Novels of Joseph Heller and Thomas Pynchon." *Adversity and Grace: Studies in Recent American Literature*. Ed. Nathan A. Scott, Jr. Chicago: U of Chicago P, 1968. 87–112. Rpt. in *Critical Essays on Thomas Pynchon*. Ed. Richard Pearce. Boston: Hall, 1981. 32–41.

Innes, Christopher. "The Salesman on the Stage: A Study in the Social Influence of Drama." *English Studies in Canada* 3.3 (1977). Rpt. in *Modern Critical Interpretations: Arthur Miller's* Death of a Salesman. Ed. Harold Bloom. New York: Chelsea, 1988. 59–75.

Irigaray, Luce. *This Sex Which Is Not One*. 1977. Trans. Catherine Porter. Ithaca: Cornell UP, 1985.

Jackson, Esther Merle. "*Death of a Salesman*: Tragic Myth in the Modern Theatre." *CLA Journal* 7.1 (1963). Rpt. in *Modern Critical Interpretations: Arthur Miller's* Death of a Salesman. Ed. Harold Bloom. New York: Chelsea, 1988. 7–18.

Jameson, Frederic. *The Political Unconscious: Narrative as Socially Symbolic Act*. Ithaca: Cornell UP, 1982.

Kharpertian, Theodore D. *A Hand to Turn the Time: The Menippean Satires of Thomas Pynchon*. Teaneck: Fairleigh Dickinson UP, 1990.

Klein, George S. *Psychoanalytic Theory: An Exploration of Essentials*. New York: International Universities, 1976.

Lacan, Jacques. "The Mirror Stage as Formative of the Function of the I." 1949. *Écrits*. 1966. Trans. Alan Sheridan. New York: Norton, 1977. 1–7.

Laing, R. D. "Ontological Insecurity." *The Divided Self*. 1959. Baltimore: Penguin, 1970. 39–61.

Lawson, Richard H. *Edith Wharton*. New York: Ungar, 1977.

LeClair, Thomas. *The Art of Excess: Mastery in Contemporary Fiction*. Urbana: U of Illinois P, 1989.

Lehan, Richard. "The Nowhere Hero." *American Dreams, American Nightmares*. Ed. David Madden. Carbondale: Southern Illinois UP, 1970. 106–14.

Lewis, Roger. "Money, Love, and Aspiration in *The Great Gatsby*." *New Essays on* The Great Gatsby. Ed. Matthew J. Bruccoli. New York: Cambridge UP, 1985. 41–57.

Lockridge, Ernest. "F. Scott Fitzgerald's *Tromp l'Oeil* and *The Great Gatsby's* Buried Plot." *Journal of Narrative Technique* 17.2 (1987): 163–83.

Luhmann, Niklas. *The Differentiation of Society*. Trans. Stephen Holmes and Charles Larmore. New York: Columbia UP, 1982.

Lukács, Georg. *History and Class Consciousness*. 1923. Trans. Rodney Livingstone. Cambridge, Mass.: MIT P, 1971.

Lyde, Marilyn Jones. *Edith Wharton: Convention and Morality in the Work of a Novelist*. Norman: U of Oklahoma P, 1959.

McDowell, Margaret B. *Edith Wharton*. Boston: Twayne, 1976.

Mangel, Anne. "Maxwell's Demon, Entropy, Information: *The Crying of Lot 49*." *TriQuarterly* 20 (1971): 194–208.

Marx, Karl. "Commodities." *Capital*. 1867. Trans. Samuel Moore and Dr. Aveling. Ed. Frederick Engels. N.p.: n.p., 1886. 1–35.

Matthiessen, F. O. *American Renaissance: Art and Expression in the Age of Emerson and Whitman*. New York: Oxford UP, 1941.

Mellard, James M. "*Something Happened*: The Imaginary, Symbolic, and the Discourse of the Family." *Critical Essays on Joseph Heller*. Ed. James Nagel. Boston: Hall, 1984. 138–55.

Merleau–Ponty, M. *Phenomenology of Perception*. 1945. Trans. Colin Smith. London: Routledge, 1962.

Merrill, Robert. *Joseph Heller*. Boston: Twayne, 1987.

Miller, Arthur. *Death of a Salesman*. 1949. *The Portable Arthur Miller*. Ed. Harold Clurman. New York: Viking, 1971. 3–133.

——. *The Theatre Essays of Arthur Miller*. Ed. Robert A. Martin. New York: Penguin, 1978.

——. *Timebends*. New York: Grove, 1987.

Mitchell, Giles. "Living and Dying for the Ideal: A Study of Willy Loman's Narcissism." *Psychoanalytic Review* 77.3 (1990): 391–407.

Montgomery, Judith H. "The American Galatia." *College English* 32 (1971): 890–98.

Moore, Benita A. *Escape into a Labyrinth: F. Scott Fitzgerald, Catholic Sensibility, and the American Way*. New York: Garland, 1988.

Moss, Leonard. *Arthur Miller*. Boston: Twayne, 1980.

Mottram, Eric. "Arthur Miller: The Development of a Political Dramatist in America." *American Theatre*. Ed. John Russell Brown and Bernard Harris. London: Arnold, 1967. Rpt. in *Arthur Miller: A Collection of Critical Essays*. Ed. Robert W. Corrigan. Englewood Cliffs: Prentice-Hall, 1969. 23–57.

Nash, Charles C. "From West Egg to Short Hills: The Decline of the Pastoral Ideal from *The Great Gatsby* to Philip Roth's *Goodbye, Columbus*." *Philological Association* 13 (1988): 22–27.

Nevius, Blake. *Edith Wharton: A Study of Her Fiction*. Berkeley: U of California P, 1953.

Norris, Frank. *McTeague*. 1899. New York: NAL, 1964.

Olsen, Lance. "Pynchon's New Nature: The Uncertainty Principle and Indeterminacy in *The Crying of Lot 49*." *Canadian Review of American Studies* 14.2 (1983): 153–63.

Överland, Orm. "Arthur Miller's Struggle with Dramatic Form." *Modern Drama* 18.1 (1975). Rpt. in *Modern Critical Views: Arthur Miller*. Ed. Harold Bloom. New York: Chelsea, 1987. 51–63.

Palmeri, Frank. "Neither Literally nor as Metaphor: Pynchon's *The Crying of Lot 49* and the Structure of Scientific Revolutions." *ELH* 54.4 (1987): 979–99.

Parker, Brian. "Point of View in Arthur Miller's *Death of a Salesman*." *University of Toronto Quarterly* 35.2 (1966): 144–57. Rpt. in *Arthur Miller: A Collection of Critical Essays*. Ed. Robert W. Corrigan. Englewood Cliffs: Prentice-Hall, 1969. 95–109.

Parker, David. "Two Versions of the Hero." *English Studies* 54.1 (1973). Rpt. in *Modern Critical Interpretations: F. Scott Fitzgerald's* The Great Gatsby. Ed. Harold Bloom. New York: Chelsea, 1986. 29–44.

Parr, Susan Resneck. "The Idea of Order at West Egg." *New Essays on* The Great Gatsby. Ed. Matthew J. Bruccoli. New York: Cambridge UP, 1985. 59–78.

Pearce, Richard. "Pynchon's Endings." *Novel: A Forum on Fiction* 18.2 (1985): 145–53.

Pease, Donald E. *Visionary Compacts: American Renaissance Writings in Cultural Context*. Madison: U of Wisconsin P, 1987.

Plath, Sylvia. "Daddy." *The Collected Poems*. 1960. New York: Harper, 1981.

Potts, Stephen W. *From Here to Absurdity: The Moral Battlefields of Joseph Heller*. San Bernadino: Borgo, 1982.

Pynchon, Thomas. *The Crying of Lot 49*. New York: Lippincott, 1966.

——. "Entropy." *Slow Learner*. 1984. New York: Bantam Windstone, 1985. 63–86.

Quilligan, Maureen. "Thomas Pynchon and the Language of Allegory." Adapted from *The Language of Allegory: Defining the Genre*. Ithaca: Cornell UP, 1979. 42–46, 204–23, 261–63, 265–78, 289–90. Rpt. in *Critical Essays on Thomas Pynchon*. Ed. Richard Pearce. Boston: Hall, 1981. 187–212.

Restuccia, Frances L. "The Name of the Lily: Edith Wharton's Feminism(s)." *Contemporary Literature* 28.2 (1987): 223–38.

Rivière, Joan. "Womanliness as Masquerade." *International Journal of Psychoanalysis* 10 (1929): 303–13.

Sartre, Jean–Paul. *Being and Nothingness*. 1943. Trans. Hazel E. Barnes. New York: Philosophical Library, 1956.

——. "The Childhood of a Leader." *The Wall and Other Stories*. 1939. Trans. Lloyd Alexander. New York: New Directions, 1948. 84–144.

——. *Nausea*. 1938. Trans. Lloyd Alexander. New York: New Directions, 1964.

——. *No Exit*. 1944. Trans. Stuart Gilbert. New York: Knopf, 1947.

Schaub, Thomas. "'A Gentle Chill, An Ambiguity': *The Crying of Lot 49.*" *Pynchon: The Voice of Ambiguity*. Urbana: U of Illinois P, 1980. 21–42. Rpt. in *Critical Essays on Thomas Pynchon*. Ed. Richard Pearce. Boston: Hall, 1981. 51–68.

Schlöndorff, Volker, dir. *Death of a Salesman*. With Dustin Hoffman, Kate Reid, John Malkovich, and Stephen Lang. Lorimar, 1986.

Schlueter, June, and James K. Flanagan. *Arthur Miller*. New York: Ungar, 1987.

Schneider, Daniel E., M.D. "Play of Dreams." *Theatre Arts* 33 (1949): 18–21.

Sebouhian, George. "From Abraham and Isaac to Bob Slocum and My Boy: Why Fathers Kill Their Sons." *Twentieth Century Literature* 27 (1981): 43–52.

Shannon, Claude E., and Warren Weaver. *The Mathematical Theory of Communication*. 1949. Urbana: U of Illinois P, 1963.

Showalter, Elaine. "The Death of the Lady (Novelist): Wharton's *House of Mirth*." *Representations* 9 (1985): 133–49.

Shulman, Robert. "Divided Selves and the Market Society: Politics and Psychology in *The House of Mirth*." *Perspectives on Contemporary Literature* 11 (1985): 10–19.

Sorkin, Adam J. "Something Happened to America: Bob Slocum and the Loss of History." *Ball State University Forum* 28.3 (1987): 35–53.

Steinberg, M. W. "Arthur Miller and the Idea of Modern Tragedy." *Dalhousie Review* 40 (1960): 329–40. Rpt. in *Arthur Miller: A Collection of Critical Essays*. Ed. Robert W. Corrigan. Englewood Cliffs: Prentice-Hall, 1969. 81–93.

Stern, Milton R. *The Golden Moment: The Novels of F. Scott Fitzgerald*. Urbana: U of Illinois P, 1970.

Strehle, Susan. "'A Permanent Game of Excuses': Determinism in Heller's *Something Happened*." *Modern Fiction Studies* 24 (1978–79): 550–56. Rpt. in *Critical Essays on Joseph Heller*. Ed. James Nagel. Boston: Hall, 1984. 106–14.

Szondi, Peter. "Memory: Miller." *Theory of Modern Drama*. Minneapolis: U of Minnesota P, 1987. 91–95. Rpt. as "Memory and Dramatic Form in *Death of a Salesman*." *Modern Critical Interpretations: Arthur Miller's* Death of a Salesman. Ed. Harold Bloom. New York: Chelsea, 1988. 19–23.

Tackács, Ferenc. "Models or Metaphors: Pattern and Paranoia in Pynchon's *Crying of Lot 49.*" *Acta Litteraria Academiae Scientiarum Hungaricae* 23.3–4 (1981): 297–306.

Tanner, Tony. *Thomas Pynchon*. New York: Methuen, 1982.

Trilling, Diana. "*The House of Mirth* Revisited." *Edith Wharton: A Collection of Critical Essays*. Ed. Irving Howe. Englewood Cliffs: Prentice-Hall, 1962. 100–118.

Trilling, Lionel. "F. Scott Fitzgerald." *The Liberal Imagination*. New York: Viking, 1950. 243–54. Rpt. in The Great Gatsby: *A Study*. Ed. Frederick J. Hoffman. New York: Scribner's, 1962. 232–43.

Troy, William. "Scott Fitzgerald—The Authority of Failure." *Accent* 6 (1945). Rpt. in *F. Scott Fitzgerald: A Collection of Critical Essays*. Ed. Arthur Mizener. Englewood Cliffs: Prentice-Hall, 1963. 20–24.

Tucker, Lindsey. "Entropy and Information Theory in Heller's *Something Happened*." *Contemporary Literature* 25 (1984): 323–40.

Urdang, Laurence, Walter W. Hunsinger, and Nancy LaRoche, eds. *Picturesque Expressions: A Thematic Dictionary*. 2nd ed. Detroit: Gale, 1985.

Vonnegut, Jr., Kurt. "*Something Happened*." Rev. of *Something Happened*, by Joseph Heller. *The New York Times Book Review* 6 Oct. 1974: 1–2. Rpt. in *Critical Essays on Joseph Heller*. Ed. James Nagel. Boston: Hall, 1984. 93–97.

Walton, Geoffrey. *Edith Wharton: A Critical Interpretation*. 2nd ed. Rutherford: Fairleigh Dickinson UP, 1982.

Ward, Dean A. "Information and the Imminent Death of Oedipa Maas." *University of Hartford Studies in Literature* 20.3 (1988): 24–37.

Watson, Robert N. "Who Bids for Tristero? The Conversion of Pynchon's Oedipa Maas." *Southern Humanities Review* 17.1 (1983): 59–75.

Way, Brian. "*The Great Gatsby*." *F. Scott Fitzgerald and the Art of Social Fiction*. London: Edward Arnold, 1980. Rpt. in *Modern Critical Interpretations: F. Scott Fitzgerald's The Great Gatsby*. Ed. Harold Bloom. New York: Chelsea, 1986. 87–108.

Weales, Gerald. "Arthur Miller's Shifting Image of Man." *The American Theatre Today*. Ed. Alan S. Downer. New York: Basic, 1967. Rpt. in *Arthur Miller: A Collection of Critical Essays*. Ed. Robert W. Corrigan. Englewood Cliffs: Prentice-Hall, 1969. 131–42.

Welland, Dennis. *Miller: A Study of His Plays*. London: Methuen, 1979.

Wershoven, Carol. *The Female Intruder in the Novels of Edith Wharton*. Rutherford: Fairleigh Dickinson UP, 1982.

Wharton, Edith. *The House of Mirth*. 1905. *Edith Wharton Novels*. New York: Library of America, 1985. 1–347.

Whitley, John S. *F. Scott Fitzgerald: The Great Gatsby*. London: Arnold, 1976.

Williams, Raymond. "Dominant, Residual, and Emergent." *Marxism and Literature*. Oxford: Oxford UP, 1977. 121–27.

——. "The Realism of Arthur Miller." *Critical Quarterly* 1 (1959): 140–49. Rpt. in *Arthur Miller: A Collection of Critical Essays*. Ed. Robert W. Corrigan. Englewood Cliffs: Prentice-Hall, 1969. 69–79.

Winnicott, D. W. "Metapsychological and Clinical Aspects of Regression within the Psycho-Analytic Setting." *Through Paediatrics to Psycho-Analysis*. New York: Basic, 1975. 278–94.

Wolff, Cynthia Griffin. *A Feast of Words: The Triumph of Edith Wharton*. New York: Oxford UP, 1977.

Index

Aarnes, William, 73
Adams, James Truslow, 5
Adorno, Theodor. *See* Horkheimer, Max,
and Theodor Adorno
Aesthetic commodity. *See* Commodity:
aesthetic
Aldridge, John W., 127, 136
Allen, Joan M., 153n. 2
Althusser, Louis, 1, 8, 79, 139
American dream: and the commodity, 5,
6–8, 41; corporate model of, 117, 120–21,
123; and empty commodity signs,
50–51, 87, 90–96, 144–46; idealization of,
5–6, 40–41; ideological armor of, 64,
69–70; woman as avatar of, 17, 19–20,
78
Ammons, Elizabeth, 152n. 1
Atkinson, Brooks, 81
Auchincloss, Louis, 152n. 1
Audhuy, Letha, 153n. 5
August, Eugene R., 154n. 4
Authorial intention, 15, 58, 82–86

Bad faith, 9, 10, 136–37, 143
Barthes, Roland, 86
Baudrillard, Jean: on postmodern culture,
91, 104, 115, 117, 137, 147; on sign-
exchange value, 6, 87, 91, 124–25,
130–31
Bauer, Dale M., 19
Bewley, Marius, 5, 6, 15, 40, 41
Bigsby, C. W. E., 81, 82
Bloom, Harold, 81
Bruccoli, Matthew, 153n. 5
Burnam, Tom, 57, 153n. 2

Canady, Nicholas, 136
Carson, Neil, 85
Carton, Evan, 116, 133
Cartwright, Kent, 40
Chase, Richard, 55
Commodification. *See* Commodity; Com-
modity psychology
Commodity, 6–7; aesthetic, 10–11, 20–23,
26–30; and history, 55, 147; and nature,
21, 59–61, 104
Commodity fetish. *See* Fetishization: of
the commodity
Commodity psychology, 7–8, 44–45,
54–55, 141–48; and sexuality, 23–26,
31–32, 49–50, 53–54, 73–80, 104–6,
127–31
Commodity sign. *See* American dream:
and empty commodity signs;
Baudrillard: on sign-exchange value
Conroy, Mark, 155n. 5
Costa, Richard Hauer, 116

Davis, Walter A., 3, 4, 25, 28, 73, 80, 137
Death: as flight from existential inward-
ness, 35–38, 71–73, 140; psychological
(death in life), 80, 122, 133–35
DelFattore, Joan, 129
Dialectical approach to literature, 12–15
Dialectical relationship of psyche and
socius, 2–3, 106–7. *See also* Existential
subjectivity, dialectical model of
Di Giuseppe, Rita, 81
Dillon, Andrew, 40, 58
Dimock, Wai-chee, 152n. 1
Dixon, Roslyn, 19

167

The Theory and Interpretation of Narrative

James Phelan and Peter J. Rabinowitz, Editors

The series publishes studies of narrative that offer interpretations of particular narratives and address significant theoretical issues underlying those interpretations. The series is interested in new interpretations of narratives to the extent that these interpretations are grounded in theoretical discussions that have implications for our understanding of narrative in general or for the interpretation of other narratives. The series does not privilege any one theoretical perspective but is open to studies from any strong theoretical position. It especially welcomes works that investigate the relations among different theoretical perspectives on narrative.

Framing *Anna Karenina*
Tolstoy, the Woman Question, and the Victorian Novel
Amy Mandelker